Two Trees
of
Knowledge

diane depper

DIANE DEKKER

TWO TREES *of* KNOWLEDGE

A Biblical Case for the Separation of School and State

TEN-WEEK BIBLE STUDY INCLUDED

Pleasant Word
PW A Division of WinePress Group

Pleasant Word (a division of WinePress Publishing, PO Box 428, Enumclaw, WA 98022) functions only as book publisher. As such, the ultimate design, content, editorial accuracy, and views expressed or implied in this work are those of the author.

Unless otherwise noted, all Scriptures are taken from the *Holy Bible, New International Version®, NIV®*. Copyright © 1973, 1978, 1984 by the International Bible Society. Used by permission of Zondervan. All rights reserved.

Scripture references marked ESV are from The Holy Bible, English Standard Version, copyright © 2001 by Crossway Bibles, a division of Good News Publishers. Used by permission. All rights reserved.

All emphasis used in Scripture verses has been added by the author.

ISBN 13: 978-1-4141-1301-2
ISBN 10: 1-4141-1301-3
Library of Congress Catalog Card Number: 2008907662

This book is dedicated first and foremost to
Jesus Christ—
in whom I live and breathe and have my being;
and secondly to my six grandchildren—
Alice, Sadie, and Kristen Keller,
daughters of Travis and Rachel Keller,
and
Katy, Meagan, and Grady Dekker,
children of Kris and Kim Dekker

Contents

Acknowledgments

MOST OF THE time spent in writing a book is time spent in solitary confinement, but it is not something one can do alone. I would like to thank my husband, Vern, who not only patiently read through my first rough drafts, but frequently came home from work to find research papers on the dinner table—and no dinner.

Thanks also to Kim Peterson, who faithfully read every chapter of the book and was my constant source of encouragement.

Thanks to Pastor Laurie Johnston, whose life exemplifies a stand for truth in a hostile culture, and who brought me to the place I needed to be to write at all.

Thanks to Pastor Kevin Schutte and his wife Kelli, for their love, hospitality, prayers, and prompting to follow the "ancient path." Thanks to the gals in my GAB (Girls and Bibles) group, who faithfully prayed me through every chapter of this book.

Thanks to my son, Kris, who motivated me to start this project in the first place, and to my daughter, Rachel, who encouraged me and gave me an insider's view of the homeschool process by faithfully homeschooling her own daughters.

Two Trees of Knowledge

Finally, thanks to my six grandchildren, who provided days of diversion and play. Every day spent with you was a holiday.

Preface

CHRISTIANS ARE AT cross purposes today on the issue of education. We all agree that a transformation of the educational system is necessary, but we disagree on how it should be accomplished. There are those who firmly believe that we should work to support the State schools by being involved in our local schools, perhaps evangelizing from within. Some have written books about how this can be done—about how parents and students can keep Christ in the classroom without breaking the law. Other Christians believe that children need to be removed from the State schools. Both sides use Scripture to support their positions, but from an ethical standpoint they cannot both be right. I applaud those teachers and other adults who have targeted the State schools as a mission field. However, I see no injunctions in Scripture that justify putting a child in this environment. It seems incongruous to me that adults who have correctly identified the mission field put their own children under the tutelage of those they believe are deficient in the knowledge of truth. Missionaries typically do not do that.

But the issue goes much deeper than that. God has given us a blueprint for transforming the culture and we are ignoring his instructions. We want to transform the culture in our own way because, quite frankly,

Two Trees of Knowledge

God's way is far too radical, not to mention politically incorrect. We want to transform the culture in a way that will not offend anyone, in a way that will personally cost us very little, if anything. This desire to do things our own way spawns disunity in the body of Christ. When we are at odds with each other, transformation of the culture is impossible. It isn't until we submit to doing things God's way, until we let him transform us, that we will transform our culture.

We have veered from the path that our forefathers walked. Our journey in the area of education has taken many dangerous detours. The secular community is daily removing every remembrance of God from the public square and the public schools. Jesus says this to the churches, "Yet I hold this against you: You have forsaken your first love. Remember the height from which you have fallen! Repent and do the things you did at first. If you do not repent, I will come to you and remove your lampstand from its place…He who has an ear, let him hear what the Spirit says to the churches. To him who overcomes, I will give the right to eat from the tree of life which is in the paradise of God" (Revelation 2:4-5, 7). If Christians are going to transform the culture, we have to reform our thinking. Without internal reformation, there will be no external transformation.

One reason there is so much disagreement on the issue of education is that many Christians are biblically illiterate. Unless we study the Bible cover to cover with these issues in mind, we will never be able to extract the principles that apply to education. It is easy to take a verse here and there and use it for our own purposes. It is much harder to study the entire Word and make comparisons between the law, the prophets, the gospels, and the apostolic letters.

Secular humanism is another subject about which Christians are sadly under-informed. We have not taken the time to study its precepts or understand its agenda. The progressives who are the greatest influence in our schools today are mostly secular humanists, and the curriculum is undergirded by a humanist philosophy. Most people believe that a secular education is a neutral education. Nothing could be further from the truth.

Secular humanism has been recognized by the United States Supreme Court as a religious worldview. It is time Christians recognize this too.

Finally, many parents have no idea what the expressed purpose of State education is. The State has an agenda that is radically different from the agenda of most parents. Parents want the best possible education for their children. The State program is not designed to give each individual the best possible education; rather, the State determines what its future needs will be, and trains its citizens to meet those needs. The State is self-serving, not parent-serving, and certainly not God-serving.

In order to right some of our misconceptions, the first four chapters of this book lay the foundation for the study of biblical principles that are found in chapters five through eight. All of us have been taken captive by the lies of our culture. We all believe things we have been taught. Without personal daily Bible study, we may not be in a position to determine truth from lies. For this reason I have also incorporated a Bible study into this book. Each of the ten chapters is followed by a five-day study for further examination of God's Word.

Parents and teachers, this book is not in any way intended as an indictment against any group of people. Most Christian parents and teachers are simply doing what they have been taught to do. However, the book is a warning. You need to be aware not only of what is happening in our culture, but why it is happening. Satan is not asleep. His intent is to steal our children. Statistics show that he is succeeding in this endeavor. The battle is for the mind. The schools are the battlefields. The children are the trophies.

Because the stakes are so high, it is not enough to merely ensure that Christian precepts are included in the secular agenda. God's displeasure with that kind of thinking is clear from 2 Kings chapter 17, where we read that the Samaritans "worshiped the LORD, but they also appointed all sorts of their own people to officiate for them as priests in the shrines at the high places. They worshiped the LORD, but they also served their own gods in accordance with the customs of the nations from which they had been brought" (verses 32-33).

America is every bit as pluralistic as ancient Samaria. God is every bit as jealous for his people today as he was in ancient times. His call to Christians today is every bit as radical as it was then: pagan institutions must be abolished—the Asherah poles must be cut down and the high places destroyed. The ancient path is not for the self-absorbed or for pleasure-seekers. It is the path that goes by way of the cross, and requires great sacrifice. In fact, it may cost everything, but the rewards are eternal.

It is my prayer that as you read this book and study God's Word, you will develop an awareness of the great cosmic battle that is taking place around us and our children, and that you will allow the Holy Spirit to guide your thinking on this critical issue of education.

Soli Deo Gloria.

Chapter 1

The Two Trees

You are free to eat from any tree in the garden; but you must not eat from the tree of the knowledge of good and evil, for when you eat of it you will surely die.

—Genesis 2:16-17

Did God really say…?

FROM THE BEGINNING of time, man has been forbidden to seek certain kinds of knowledge. In the middle of the Garden of Eden, God planted two trees, the tree of life and the tree of the knowledge of good and evil. The knowledge imparted by the fruit of these trees determined the consumers' eternal destiny. One tree bestowed knowledge leading to eternal life: "Now this is eternal life: that they may *know* you, the only true God, and Jesus Christ, whom you have sent" (John 17:3). The other tree provided knowledge that brought spiritual death. God warned Adam and Eve not to eat of that tree; if they did, they would die. Yet the serpent persuaded Eve to partake of it. Why did she do it? Quite frankly, she didn't want someone else deciding what was good for her. She wanted to determine that for herself. She wanted to be God.

Additionally, she had the assurance of the serpent, "You will not surely die." Believing the lie, she consumed the fruit that poisoned her soul. Afterward, she gave some to Adam, who was standing with her. He too ate of the poisoned fruit, thus infecting his offspring forever.

That day God and Satan became locked in a cosmic battle that has continued through the ages, affecting every one of us. The trophies in this battle are the minds and souls of men. In his book *Children at Risk,* James Dobson noted:

> Nothing short of a great Civil War of Values rages today throughout North America. Two sides with vastly differing and incompatible worldviews are locked in a bitter conflict that permeates every level of society… Instead of fighting for territory or military conquest, however, the struggle now is for the hearts and minds of the people. It is a war over ideas. And someday soon, I believe, a winner will emerge and the loser will fade from memory…[1]

What goes into the mind of a man directly affects his soul, bringing spiritual life or spiritual death. No wonder then, that the primary ground on which this battle is waged is in the schools. Satan doesn't care about how cute our children are or how much we love them. He passionately hates them, and like a lion seeking to devour its prey, he seeks to separate our children from God and us forever. He is succeeding.

Recent studies by independent Christian organizations such as the Nehemiah Institute,[2] the Southern Baptist Convention, and the Josh McDowell ministry are showing that as many as 75%-90% of Christian students who are educated in the public school system are rejecting the faith of their parents. The Barna Research Group, a marketing research company specializing in cultural trends and the Christian church, reports that only 9% of all teenagers in the U.S. are certain that there is absolute moral truth. That percentage is not significantly higher for those who go to church. The group also found that in many cases children attending church are not instructed on how to discern God's truth or given a proper perspective on Scripture. Families are faring no better. According to Barna, less than ten percent of Christian families spend time in Bible reading and prayer, other than prayer at mealtime. Many Christian students coming out of the public schools believe that Christianity is merely a personal preference that has no meaning for their daily lives. To many students, the Bible is out of touch with the reality of life *as they experience it*. Therefore, they either reject it altogether, or they try to make it conform to their own reality. One earmark of this emerging generation is the tendency to interpret the Bible in light of the culture rather than interpreting the culture in light of the Bible. This adulterated Christianity is no Christianity at all.

As Christian parents, the single most important job we have is to raise our children to be godly men and women. Malachi 2:15 says, "Has not the LORD made them [marriage partners] one? In flesh and spirit they are his. And why one? *Because he was seeking godly offspring.*" The eternal welfare of our children must be the highest priority of our lives. By the time our children leave home, the Word of God should dwell in them richly. They should have memorized stories from the Bible, and be thoroughly trained in ferreting out biblical principles and applying them to activities of daily life such as finding a mate, managing household budgets, educating and disciplining children, working, voting, and serving their churches and communities. They should also be able to articulately defend their faith to an unbelieving world.

Paul says in 2 Corinthians 10:5, "We demolish arguments and every pretension that sets itself up against the knowledge of God, and we take captive every thought to make it obedient to Christ." Teaching our children to take captive *every* thought to make it obedient to Christ is a monumental task that requires twenty-four-hour-a-day training and vigilance. God has entrusted the children to us, assigned us to be the keepers of our children's minds. Consider this: Parents who make provision for their children in the event of their own deaths do not entrust their children to just anybody. They seek parents they trust implicitly, who will raise their children in precisely the way they've instructed, down to the last detail. In the same way, God has given his children to Christian parents, entrusting them with a responsibility to follow his instructions down to the last detail. Those who have had their children baptized or dedicated in a formal service have vowed to carry out these instructions to the best of their ability. Christ has given parents the honor of leading children to him. He gives us the same injunction he gave the apostle Peter: Feed my lambs.

A shepherd nurtures and protects his sheep. He makes sure they are well fed and keeps them away from things that would poison or harm them. In the Garden of Eden, God gave a clear command about knowledge. Certain kinds of knowledge poison the soul. Arguments and pretensions that set themselves up "against the knowledge of God" are such poisons (2 Corinthians 10:5). The knowledge that brings life is the knowledge of God. Our task then, as parents, is to indoctrinate our children in the knowledge of God, *while protecting them from indoctrination in the "arguments" that set themselves up "against the knowledge of God."* As he commanded Eve so long ago, God commands us today to be not conformed to the pattern of this world, but to be transformed *by the renewing of our minds* (Romans 12:2). There are only two kinds of knowledge—one brings life, the other death. There is no neutral ground.

Jesus himself left no room for neutrality; he forced the world to take sides when he said, "He who is not with me is against me, and he who does not gather with me scatters" (Matthew 12:30). While standing before Pilate, Jesus said, "for this reason I was born, to testify to the truth. *Everyone on the side of truth* listens to me" (John 18:37). Apart from Christ there is no truth. Knowledge divorced from God is not neutral, it is against Christ. Still, many Christians today have bought into the cultural belief that this kind of knowledge is safe.

To better understand why this happens, we need to understand the concept of worldview and how it influences our perception of the world and reality. Our worldview is like a lens through which we see the universe. As we look through this lens, we make determinations about what is real and what is not, what is true and what is not. Nancy Pearcey, author of *Total Truth,* defines it this way: "A worldview is like a mental map that tells us how to navigate the world effectively…each of us carries a model of the universe inside our heads that tells us what the world is like and how we should live in it."[3] A worldview can also be seen as a set of presuppositions by which we live. The importance of worldview becomes apparent when we realize that our worldview is the determinant of all of our behavior. Francis Schaeffer writes:

> People have presuppositions, and they will live more consistently on the basis of these presuppositions than even they themselves may realize. By *presuppositions* we mean the basic way an individual looks at life, his basic world view, the grid through which he sees the world. Presuppositions rest upon that which a person considers to be the truth of what exists. People's presuppositions lay a grid for all they bring forth into the external world. Their presuppositions also provide the basis for their values and therefore the basis for all their decisions.

> "As a man thinketh, so is he," is really most profound. An individual is not just the product of the forces around him. He has a mind, an inner world. Then, having thought, a person can bring forth actions into the external world and thus influence it. People are apt to look at the outer theater of action, forgetting the actor who "lives in the mind" and who therefore is the true actor in the external world. The inner thought world determines the outward action.[4]

Many people see Christianity as nothing more than a plan of salvation, and lack any sense of how Christianity functions as a unified, comprehensive system of truth that applies to social issues, politics, economics, and education as well as religion. They mistakenly presume to have a biblical worldview because they believe in God and the Bible. While they are sincere about their faith, they have adopted their views on just about everything else from their education, the media, and their next-door neighbors.

Two Trees of Knowledge

Our worldviews are infused into us by those who instruct us. The purpose of education is to teach us about the world we live in—what is real and what is not real—and how to pattern our thinking and actions to accommodate that reality. In other words, the purpose of education is to train the mind in a particular worldview. Once that worldview has been established, every new piece of information we acquire will be seen through that lens, and interpreted accordingly. Science, mathematics, history, geography, social studies, literature, religion, and language are the foundations of our worldview. Our educators answer such questions as: What is true about the world? What must we know to survive? How did life originate? Who is man? Who is God? What is our purpose? Where are we going? What are our roots? Is there absolute truth? Are all values equal? If education in the public schools answers these questions—*and it does*—then there can be no doubt that its professed neutrality is a lie.

An objection that arises in reference to neutrality is that facts are facts, so it makes no difference whether you learn them in a public school or a Christian school. Two times two equals four no matter where you learn it. But what is the basis for being able to know that two times two equals four? The ultimate point of reference and meaning is not the same for a believer as for an unbeliever. Cornelius Van Til, best known as professor of apologetics at Westminster Theological Seminary, explains:

> Now the fact that two times two are four does not mean the same thing to you as a believer and to someone else as an unbeliever. When you think of two times two as four, you connect this fact with numerical law. And when you connect this fact with numerical law, you must connect numerical law with all law. The question you face, then, is whether law exists in its own right or is an expression of the will and nature of God. Thus the fact that two times two are four enables you to implicate yourself more deeply into the nature and will of God. On the other hand, when an unbeliever says two times two are four, he will also be led to connect this fact with the whole idea of law; but he will regard this law as independent of God. Thus the fact that

two times two are four enables him, so he thinks, to get farther away from God. That fact will place the unbeliever before a whole sea of open possibilities in which he may seek to realize his life away from God...[5]

An unbeliever who sees the law as independent from God recognizes no relationship between himself and his environment. How can he stand in relationship to an impersonal law? He will eventually make himself a god, and take credit for making the law himself. Nancy Pearcey notes that modern man has done just that. She points out that American school children are now taught a postmodern view of math. A popular middle school curriculum says students should learn that "mathematics is man-made, that it is arbitrary, and good solutions are arrived at by consensus among those who are considered expert."[6] Students who are taught that mathematics is man-made may not think about it at the time, but the philosophical poison will take root and bear fruit down the road. C.S. Lewis addresses this phenomenon in *The Abolition of Man* where he says,

> I doubt whether we are sufficiently attentive to the importance of elementary textbooks...The very power of [schoolmasters] depends on the fact that they are dealing with a boy: a boy who thinks he is "doing" his "English prep" and has no notion that ethics, theology, and politics are all at stake. It is not theory they put into his mind, but an assumption, which ten years hence, its origin forgotten and its presence unconscious, will condition him to take one side in a controversy which he has never recognized as a controversy at all.[7]

A math curriculum in current use in our country is a perfect example of how this phenomenon is played out. "Radical math," part of a broader social justice curriculum, integrates issues of social and economic justice into the math curriculum. Classroom projects train students to see social problems from a radical anti-capitalist perspective.

Two Trees of Knowledge

The kids think they are merely doing math, but all the while they are being indoctrinated in socialist philosophy. Therein lies the danger; their minds are being trained to conform to the worldview of the curriculum. *It is the worldview, not the facts, that leads to spiritual blindness.*

Because many parents do not understand the role that worldview plays in education, they naïvely assume that they can let the school be responsible for head knowledge, while they assume responsibility for the heart by adding religious instruction. However, Louis Berkhof, president of Calvin Theological Seminary from 1931 to 1944, illustrates the impossibility of separating what goes into the head from what goes into the heart. He writes,

> We are constantly reminded of the fact that it is the whole man that perceives and thinks, that desires and wills. Consequently his education should also be regarded as a unitary process. It is utter folly to think that you can inform the intellect without giving direction to the will, that you store the head with knowledge without affecting the emotions, the inclinations, the desires, and the aspirations of the heart. The training of the head and of the heart go together, and in both the fundamental fact that the child is the image bearer of God must be a determining factor. Again, in view of the fact that education is and should be a unitary process, we understand the absolute absurdity of saying that the school is only concerned with the head and should limit itself to secular education, while the home and church make provision for the heart by adding religious education. We should never forget that the education a child receives in the school, though divorced from religion, is nevertheless an education of the entire child and is bound to make a deep impression on the heart.[8]

Berkhof goes on to say that because the soul is a unit, and education is a unitary process, it is of utmost importance that the home, church, and school share the same conception of the essential nature of the child. An education that proceeds in part on the assumption that God exists, and in part on the supposition that God does not exist or that if he does he is irrelevant, can never result in a life that is truly unified. Partaking from the fruit of both trees leads to a divided life, and produces people who are "swayed and torn by conflicting opinions, lacking in singleness of purpose, in stability and strength, and in that true joy that fills the soul and is constantly moving in the right direction."[9]

The divided life that Berkhof refers to is the result of trying to synthesize two incompatible worldviews. If we compare our worldview to a lens, then we have two lenses to choose from, either the lens of truth (the biblical worldview) or the lens of the world. The problem with looking at the world through its own lens is that that lens filters out the truth. For example, in view of promoting diversity, children from very young ages are introduced to homosexuality as an alternative lifestyle. They are taught that homosexuality is normal and that families can be headed by two members of the same sex. They are given books to read that have homosexual protagonists with whom they identify emotionally. These characters are portrayed as intelligent, witty, beautiful, and downtrodden. Students may know homosexual teachers and other students who are homosexual. From the world's perspective, homosexuals are no different from heterosexuals except for their sexual preference. Is this the truth? From a biblical perspective, it is not.

The Bible teaches that homosexuality is an abomination. When we examine the homosexual cult through the biblical lens, we find out why. Thirty percent of homosexual men do not live to see their thirtieth birthday.[10] Most of those who make it into their forties are so disease-ridden that they are unable to find and keep partners. Many become predators who prey on young healthy boys. The average homosexual has 254 sexual encounters during a lifetime, and no life-long partner.[11] He will never experience the joys of children or grandchildren and will most likely die alone. Homosexuality is not a lifestyle, it is a deathstyle. This information is not disseminated in the schools. The lens the world looks through is a lens that blinds its viewer to the truth. What happens to a student who follows a blind teacher? Jesus says this, "Can a blind man lead a blind man? Will they not both fall into a pit? A student is not above his teacher, *but everyone who is fully trained will be like his teacher*" (Luke 6:39-40).

Most children are not going to take the time to research the truth about homosexuality on their own, so all they really know is what they hear and see at school or on TV. They end up confused because what the Bible says doesn't match their personal experience. They do not realize that their personal experiences have been carefully structured to shield them from the truth. They believe the lie, and this is where the danger lurks. All sin begins with believing a lie.

In nearly every subject, textbooks present the cultural worldview as reality, while making the biblical worldview look ridiculous. There is only one conclusion we can draw from this: the public education system in America is a snare to covenant children. It is a tree producing poisonous fruit that leads to spiritual death.

Soli Deo Gloria

FURTHER UP
AND
FURTHER IN

WEEK ONE—DAY ONE

God's Children

KNOWLEDGE:

Genesis 4:1

Adam lay with his wife Eve, and she became pregnant and gave birth to Cain. She said, "With the help of the LORD I have brought forth a man."

Genesis 4:25

Adam lay with his wife again, and she gave birth to a son and named him Seth, saying, "God has granted me another child in place of Abel, since Cain killed him."

Genesis 17:16

I will bless her and will surely give you a son by her. I will bless her so that she will be the mother of nations; kings of peoples will come from her."

Genesis 28:3

May God Almighty bless you and make you fruitful and increase your numbers until you become a community of peoples.

Genesis 30:6

Then Rachel said, "God has vindicated me; he has listened to my plea and given me a son." Because of this she named him Dan.

Psalm 133:9

He settles the barren woman in her home as the happy mother of children. Praise the LORD.

Psalm 127:3-5

Sons are a heritage from the LORD, children a reward from him. Like arrows in the hands of a warrior are sons born in one's youth. Blessed is the man whose quiver is full of them.

1 Corinthians 7:14

For the unbelieving husband has been sanctified through his wife, and the unbelieving wife has been sanctified through her believing husband. Otherwise, your children would be unclean, but as it is they are holy.

Malachi 2:15

Has not the LORD made them one? In flesh and spirit, they are his. And why one? Because he was seeking godly offspring.

Ezekiel 18:4

For every living soul belongs to me, the father as well as the son—both alike belong to me.

1 Corinthians 6:19

If we live, we live to the Lord, and if we die, we die to the Lord. So, whether we live or die, we belong to the Lord.

UNDERSTANDING:

1. Who ultimately decides whether or not we will have children?
2. To whom do our children belong?
3. For what purposes does God give us children?

WISDOM:

What are the implications of this as we consider how to train and educate our children?

NOTES

_____

_____

_____

_____

_____

_____

_____

_____

_____

_____

_____

_____

_____

_____

Week One—Day Two

A Trust

KNOWLEDGE:

1 Timothy 6:20

Timothy, guard what has been entrusted to your care. Turn away from godless chatter and the opposing ideas of what is falsely called knowledge.

1 Corinthians 4:2

Now it is required that those who have been given a trust must prove faithful.

Matthew 18:10-14

See that you do not look down on one of these little ones. For I tell you that their angels in heaven always see the face of my Father in heaven. What do you think? If a man owns a hundred sheep, and one of them wanders away, will he not leave the ninety-nine on the hills and go to look for the one that wandered off? And if he finds it, I tell you the truth, he is happier about that one sheep than about the ninety-nine that did not wander off. In the same way your Father in heaven is not willing that any of these little ones should be lost.

Mark 10:13-16

People were bringing little children to Jesus to have him touch them, but the disciples rebuked them. When Jesus saw this, he was indignant. He said to them, "Let the little children come to me, and do not hinder them, for the kingdom of God belongs to such as these. I tell you the truth, anyone who will not receive the kingdom of God like a little child will never enter it." And he took the children in his arms, put his hands on them and blessed them.

Matthew 18:6

But if anyone causes one of these little ones who believe in me to sin, it would be better for him to have a large millstone hung around his neck and to be drowned in the depths of the sea.

UNDERSTANDING:

1. When God commanded Adam and Eve not to eat the fruit from the tree of the knowledge of good and evil, he was protecting them from counterfeit truth claims (lies). How is Paul's injunction to Timothy based on the same principle?
2. How do Jesus' statements in Mark 10 and Matthew 18 confirm the principle that the children of believers are set apart for him?

WISDOM:

1. Timothy was entrusted with discipling those who were members of the church he was shepherding. Part of his job was to protect the flock from "what is falsely called knowledge." How do these verses apply to parents who have been entrusted with discipling God's children?
2. How do lies or false truth claims hinder a child from coming to Jesus?
3. Give some examples of how parents can remove the hindrances that might prevent children from believing the lies of our culture.

NOTES

_____

_____

_____

_____

_____

_____

_____

_____

_____

_____

_____

_____

_____

_____

_____

_____

WEEK ONE—DAY THREE

Teaching the Children

KNOWLEDGE:

Deuteronomy 6:4-9

Hear, O Israel: The LORD our God, the LORD is one. Love the LORD your God with all your heart and with all your soul and with all your strength. These commandments that I give you today are to be upon your hearts. Impress them on your children. Talk about them when you sit at home and when you walk along the road, when you lie down and when you get up. Tie them as symbols on your hands and bind them on your foreheads. Write them on the doorframes of your houses and on your gates.

Deuteronomy 11:18-21

Fix these words of mine in your hearts and minds; tie them as symbols on your hands and bind them on your foreheads. Teach them to your children, talking about them when you sit at home and when you walk along the road, when you lie down and when you get up. Write them on the doorframes of your houses and on your gates, so that your days and the days of your children may be many in the land that the LORD swore to give your forefathers, as many as the days that the heavens are above the earth.

Psalm 78:1-7

O my people, hear my teaching; listen to the words of my mouth. I will open my mouth in parables, I will utter hidden things, things from of old—what we have heard and known, what our fathers have told us. We will not hide them from their children; we will tell the next generation the praiseworthy deeds of the LORD, his power, and the wonders he has done. He decreed statutes for Jacob and established the law in Israel, which he commanded our forefathers to teach their children, so the next generation would know them, even the children yet to be born, and they in turn would tell their children. Then they would put their trust in God and would not forget his deeds but would keep his commands.

Ephesians 6:4

Fathers, do not exasperate your children; instead, bring them up in the training and instruction of the Lord.

UNDERSTANDING:

1. According to these passages, whom does God ultimately hold responsible for training and educating children?
2. God's instructions to the Israelites included all areas of knowledge—from diet and hygiene to treating mold and mildew, to regulation of business and charging interest, and agricultural science. This would have involved teaching the children reading, mathematics, science, medicine, law, and so forth. Discuss how our culture today perpetrates the lie that these subjects are religiously/philosophically neutral.

WISDOM:

Louis Berkhof suggested that education in two worldviews produces people who are "swayed and torn by conflicting opinions, lacking in singleness of purpose." How does Ephesians 6:4 address this?

NOTES

_____

_____

_____

_____

_____

_____

_____

_____

_____

_____

_____

_____

_____

_____

WEEK ONE—DAY FOUR

Twenty-four/Seven

KNOWLEDGE:

Deuteronomy 6:4-9

Hear, O Israel: The LORD our God, the LORD is one. Love the LORD your God with all your heart and with all your soul and with all your strength. These commandments that I give you today are to be upon your hearts. Impress them on your children. Talk about them when you sit at home and when you walk along the road, when you lie down and when you get up. Tie them as symbols on your hands and bind them on your foreheads. Write them on the doorframes of your houses and on your gates.

Psalm 1:1-2

Blessed is the man
who does not walk in the counsel of the wicked
or stand in the way of sinners
or sit in the seat of mockers.

But his delight is in the law of the LORD,
 and on his law he meditates day and night.

2 Corinthians 10:5

We demolish arguments and every pretension that sets itself up against the knowledge of God, and we take captive *every thought* to make it obedient to Christ.

Psalm 119:97-104

Oh, how I love your law!
I meditate on it all day long.

Your commands make me wiser than my enemies,
for they are ever with me.

I have more insight than all my teachers,
for I meditate on your statutes.

I have more understanding than the elders,
for I obey your precepts.

I have kept my feet from every evil path
so that I might obey your word.

I have not departed from your laws,
for you yourself have taught me.

How sweet are your words to my taste,
sweeter than honey to my mouth!

I gain understanding from your precepts;
therefore I hate every wrong path.

UNDERSTANDING:

1. How many hours of each day are we to meditate on God's precepts?
2. How much time should parents spend each day talking to their children and modeling Christian behavior for them?

WISDOM:

1. In the event that a parent cannot attend to the children all day long, to whom should they delegate the responsibility of consistently teaching and modeling Christian behavior?
2. Suggest ways parents can control the environment of their children on a 24/7 basis.

NOTES

_____

_____

_____

_____

_____

_____

_____

_____

_____

_____

_____

_____

_____

_____

_____

_____

WEEK ONE—DAY FIVE

Consequences

KNOWLEDGE:

Genesis 2:15-17

The LORD God took the man and put him in the Garden of Eden to work it and take care of it. And the LORD God commanded the man, "You are free to eat from any tree in the garden; but you must not eat from the tree of the knowledge of good and evil, for when you eat of it you will surely die."

Proverbs 1:28-33

"Then they will call to me but I will not answer;
they will look for me but will not find me.

Since they hated knowledge
and did not choose to fear the LORD,

since they would not accept my advice
and spurned my rebuke,

they will eat the fruit of their ways
and be filled with the fruit of their schemes.

For the waywardness of the simple will kill them,
and the complacency of fools will destroy them;

but whoever listens to me will live in safety
and be at ease, without fear of harm."

Hosea 4:6

My people are destroyed from lack of knowledge.
Because you have rejected knowledge,
I also reject you as my priests;
because you have ignored the law of your God,
I also will ignore your children.

Matthew 16:11-12

"How is it you don't understand that I was not talking to you about bread? But be on your guard against the yeast of the Pharisees and Sadducees." Then they understood that he was not telling them to guard against the yeast used in bread, but against the teaching of the Pharisees and Sadducees.

Ephesians 4:18

They [Gentiles] are darkened in their understanding and separated from the life of God because of the ignorance that is in them due to the hardening of their hearts.

UNDERSTANDING:

1. How do we know that God's command to Adam and Eve in the Garden still applies to us today?
2. What does God say about children in Hosea 4:6?
3. What kind of teaching does Jesus warn about?

WISDOM:

1. Counterfeit knowledge is to the soul like arsenic is to the body. How does knowing that affect what we should listen to, read, and watch on TV? Can a whole lot of good food counter the effects of the poison?

2. Assuming that moving to the desert and living in a cave is not an option, how can Christian parents best protect their families from the assaults of our culture?

NOTES

_____

_____

_____

_____

_____

_____

_____

_____

_____

_____

_____

_____

_____

_____

Chapter 2

Humanism: A Counterfeit Worldview

Then they said, "Come, let us build ourselves a city with a tower that reaches to the heavens, so that we may make a name for ourselves and not be scattered over the face of the earth."

—Genesis 11:4

ISRAEL WAS CONSTANTLY ensnared by its neighboring nations into worshipping other gods. God had commanded them to completely destroy the nations they conquered—not just the men, but the women and children also. Before they even reached Canaan, God warned them about their relationships with heathen nations:

Obey what I command you today. I will drive out before you the Amorites, Canaanites, Hittites, Perizzites, Hivites and Jebusites. *Be careful not to make a treaty with those who live in the land where you are going, or they will be a snare among you. Break down their altars, smash their sacred stones and cut down their Asherah poles.* Do not worship any other god, for the LORD, whose name is Jealous, is a jealous God.

Be careful not to make a treaty with those who live in the land; for when they prostitute themselves to their gods and sacrifice to them, they will invite you and you will eat their sacrifices. And when you choose some of their daughters as wives for your sons and those daughters prostitute themselves to their gods, they will lead your sons to do the same.

—Exodus 34:11-16

During Joshua's lifetime, the Israelites obeyed and God blessed them, but when Joshua died they failed to follow God's commands. They repeatedly prostituted themselves, embracing the gods and customs of the nations around them. The ten northern tribes worshipped golden calves made by King Jeroboam. After that, Israel never again had a godly king. Judah had only a few. By the time of Jeremiah the prophet, there was virtually no knowledge of God in the land. God spoke to Jeremiah:

"Beware of your friends; do not trust your brothers. For every brother is a deceiver, and every friend a slanderer. Friend deceives friend, and no one speaks the truth...*You live in the midst of deception; in their deceit they refuse to acknowledge me," declares the* LORD.

—Jeremiah 9:4-6

Yet God did not give up on Israel. Even then, when all seemed lost, God pleaded with his people not to eat of the tree that would poison their souls: *"Do not learn the ways of the nations...*for the customs of the peoples are worthless" (Jeremiah 10:2-3).

The "human tradition" (Colossians 2:8) the Bible warns us about so explicitly, manifests itself in many ways, but its objective is the exaltation of man and the rejection of God. Secular humanism is the prevailing manifestation of this deadly tradition in our culture. We may think that because it embraces no God, it is a religiously neutral philosophy. We may think that because secular humanists have no church, they are not organized. However, the United States Supreme Court has not only recognized secular humanists as an organized group, but has given them the same tax-exempt status as churches and other charitable organizations. Because we tend to underestimate the enemy, we need to retrace the history of humanism, and review its major precepts.

Humanism was the original sin in the Garden of Eden. Eve sought to exalt herself and throw off God's rules, to determine for herself what was good and evil. Man's rebellion against God continued, and Old Testament humanism reached its zenith at the Tower of Babel. Here men gathered together to build a city and a tower that would reach to the heavens in defiance of God. Their purpose was to make a name for themselves, and not be scattered over the whole earth as God had commanded. The tower that reached to the heavens was their security in the event of another flood. God wasn't going to destroy them a second time! But God intervened and scattered them by confusing their language. (See Genesis 11)

The history of humanism throughout the ages is the story of human defiance against God. Francis Schaeffer's *How Then Should We Live?* is a comprehensive history of humanism and its effects on world culture, which gives us a broad understanding of just how destructive this philosophy is. We will examine a brief synopsis of this history.

The Greeks and the Hebrews are the two ancient cultures that represent the contrast between the biblical and humanist worldviews. The Greek culture epitomized the expression of humanism and humanistic thought. Although Greece was the birthplace of human rights and democracy, secular historians wrongly credit the Greeks with providing the foundations for American government. The foundations of American government come directly from the Hebrew tradition in which the Creator is the giver of rights and government is under the authority of God. Embedded within the Hebrew writings were the very words of God. God had given instructions to the Hebrews that encompassed every area of life—marriage and family, personal relationships, health and hygiene, business practices, religious practices, and government. Our judicial, legislative, and executive branches of government are based directly on God's role as judge, lawgiver, and king. "For the LORD is our judge, the LORD is our lawgiver, the LORD is our king; it is he who will save us" (Isaiah 33:22).

The early church had the advantage of the New Testament writings to help clarify the biblical worldview and illustrate how to put biblical principles into practice. As Christianity became the dominant religion of Europe, the biblical worldview became predominant in Western civilization. However, during the fourteenth, fifteenth, and sixteenth centuries, the Renaissance brought forth a rebirth in the ideas about man. Renaissance humanism celebrated human autonomy, and its value system was rooted in the belief that man is his own measure. This change of philosophy once again put man at the center of all things. As humanism crept into the early church, the authority of the church rivaled the authority of biblical teaching. More emphasis was placed on man's works than on Christ's work. Many distortions in teaching and in practice resulted. The church had already been primed for this change in thinking because of the writings of Thomas Aquinas, who believed that the fall of man affected man's will, but not his intellect. According to Aquinas, human wisdom could be trusted, resulting in the belief that faith could as readily be put in worldly philosophers as in Scripture. An increasing synthesis between biblical teaching and pagan thought brought the Catholic Church farther and farther away from the truths of Christianity.

Martin Luther, John Calvin, and other reformers returned to a more pristine Christianity using Scripture as the sole authority for daily living. To these reformers, the church was not equal to or above the authority of Scripture, but under it. Their motto was *Sola Scriptura—the Scriptures only.* The goal of the Reformation was to remove the humanistic distortions which had infiltrated the church. Martin Luther translated the Bible into German, making it available to the laity. Calvin wrote his *Institutes of the Christian Religion.*

Although the Reformation did not bring about social perfection, it did offer society the opportunity to experience tremendous freedom because of the consensus of the governed to live under the principles of biblical authority. Without this consensus, freedom results in utter chaos. The Bible provided the basis not only of morals, but of law. With the spread of the Reformation, Europeans began to experience for the first time the truth that true freedom can only exist within the context of Christianity.

The change in England became known as the "Bloodless Revolution." William of Orange 3 and Mary were the reigning monarchs (1688) when Parliament became an equal partner with the crown. This allowed for deliberate control of the monarchy by the people. All of Europe was impacted by the resulting freedoms of the English. The French philosopher Voltaire, often called the "father of the Enlightenment," wrote in his *Letters Concerning the English Nation,* "The English are the only people upon earth who have been able to prescribe limits to the power of Kings by resisting them, and who, by a series of struggles, have at last established…that wise government where the prince is all powerful to do good, and at the same time is restrained from committing evil…and where the people share in the government without confusion."[12] Even so, Voltaire himself was a committed humanist whose Enlightenment beliefs were the antithesis of Reformation thought.

When the French Revolution tried to reproduce the experience of the English, it rejected Reformation principles. Based on Voltaire's Enlightenment principles, the result was a bloodbath, a breakdown of government, and ensuing chaos. In September 1792 a massacre of 1,300 prisoners took place and before it was over, the government and its agents killed 40,000 people, many of them innocent peasants. The parallels between this revolution and the later Russian revolution are remarkable. Revolutions with a purely humanist base have only two options: anarchy or repression. Francis Schaeffer notes, "what the Reformation produced…is all in gigantic contrast to what the Communist countries continue to produce. Marxist-Leninist Communists have a great liability in arguing their case because so far in no place have the Communists gained and continued in power, building on their materialistic base, without repressive policies."[13]

Today, humanism takes on a variety of forms, but the most prevalent in American culture is secular humanism followed by Marxism/Leninism.

Two Trees of Knowledge

Our government and our schools are fighting to take every reference to God out of the public arena and public textbooks. They have already succeeded with the textbooks. More than thirty years ago, Schaeffer stated, "In our era, sociologically, man destroyed the base which gave him the possibility of freedoms without chaos. Humanists have been determined to beat to death the knowledge of God and the knowledge that God has not been silent, but has spoken in the Bible and through Christ—and they have been determined to do this even though the death of values has come with the death of that knowledge."[14] Jeremiah's words ring true today: "'You live in the midst of deception; in their deceit they refuse to acknowledge Me,' declares the LORD" (Jeremiah 9:6).

The humanist manifestos outline the basic beliefs of humanism. Humanist Manifesto 1 was written in 1933, and was written in part by John Dewey, known as the father of progressive education. Humanist Manifesto 2 was written about forty years later and signed by writers, university professors, feminists, pro-abortionists, psychologists, and others who profoundly impacted education in the United States. The last manifesto, Humanist Manifesto 2000, adds a global vision to the spread of humanism, which in effect brings us full circle from the Tower of Babel. Here are some condensed passages from the Humanist Manifesto 2:[15]

Preface

As in 1933, **humanists still believe that traditional theism**, especially faith in the prayer-hearing God, assumed to live and care for persons, to hear and understand their prayers, and to be able to do something about them, **is an unproved and outmoded faith. Salvationism, based on mere affirmation, still appears as harmful, diverting people with false hopes of heaven hereafter. Reasonable minds look to other means for survival.**

Traditional moral codes and newer irrational cults both fail to meet the pressing needs of today and tomorrow. **False "theologies of hope"**

and messianic ideologies, substituting new dogmas for old, **cannot cope with existing world realities**. They separate rather than unite peoples.

Religion

We believe, however, that traditional dogmatic or authoritarian religions that place revelation, God, ritual, or creed above human needs and experience do a disservice to the human species. Any account of nature should pass the tests of scientific evidence; in our judgment, the dogmas and myths of traditional religions do not do so. Even at this late date in human history, certain elementary facts based upon the critical use of scientific reason have to be restated. **We find insufficient evidence for belief in the existence of a supernatural; it is either meaningless or irrelevant to the question of survival and fulfillment of the human race. As non-theists, we begin with humans not God, nature not deity.** Nature may indeed be broader and deeper than we now know; any new discoveries, however, will but enlarge our knowledge of the natural.

We appreciate the need to preserve the best ethical teachings in the religious traditions of humankind, many of which we share in common. But we reject those features of traditional religious morality that deny humans a full appreciation of their own potentialities and responsibilities. ...**But we can discover no divine purpose or providence for the human species. While there is much that we do not know, humans are responsible for what we are or will become. No deity will save us; we must save ourselves.**

Promises of immortal salvation or fear of eternal damnation are both illusory and harmful. ...Rather, science affirms that the human species is an emergence from natural evolutionary forces. As far as we know, the total personality is a function of the biological organism transacting in a social and cultural context. **There is no credible evidence that life survives the death of the body.** We continue to exist in our progeny and in the way that our lives have influenced others in our culture.

Ethics

We affirm that moral values derive their source from human experience. Ethics is autonomous and situational needing no theological or ideological sanction. Ethics stems from human need and interest. To deny this distorts the whole basis of life. Human life has meaning because we create and develop our futures. Happiness and the creative realization of human needs and desires, individually and in shared enjoyment, are continuous themes of humanism. We strive for the good life, here and now. The goal is to pursue life's enrichment despite debasing forces of vulgarization, commercialization, and dehumanization.

The Individual

In the area of sexuality, we believe that intolerant attitudes, often cultivated by orthodox religions and puritanical cultures, unduly repress sexual conduct. The right to birth control, abortion, and divorce should be recognized. While we do not approve of exploitive, denigrating forms of sexual expression, **neither do we wish to prohibit, by law or social sanction, sexual behavior between consenting adults.** The many varieties of sexual exploration should not in themselves be considered "evil."

Democratic Society

To enhance freedom and dignity the individual must experience a full range of civil liberties in all societies. This includes freedom of speech and the press, political democracy, the legal right of opposition to governmental policies, fair judicial process, religious liberty, freedom of association, and artistic, scientific, and cultural freedom. **It also includes a recognition of an individual's right to die with dignity, euthanasia, and the right to suicide.** We oppose the increasing invasion of privacy, by whatever means, in both totalitarian and democratic societies. We would safeguard, extend, and implement the principles of human freedom evolved from the Magna Carta to the Bill of Rights, the Rights of Man, and the Universal Declaration of Human Rights.

We are committed to an open and democratic society. We must extend participatory democracy in its true sense to the economy, the school, the family, the workplace, and voluntary associations. Decision-making must be decentralized to include widespread involvement of people at all levels — social, political, and economic. All persons should have a voice in developing the values and goals that determine their lives. Institutions should be responsive to expressed desires and needs. The conditions of work, education, devotion, and play should be humanized. **Alienating forces should be modified or eradicated and bureaucratic structures should be held to a minimum. People are more important than decalogues [ten commandments], rules, proscriptions, or regulations.**

The separation of church and state and the separation of ideology and state are imperatives. The state should encourage maximum freedom for different moral, political, religious, and social values in society. **It should not favor any particular religious bodies** through the use of public monies, **nor espouse a single ideology and function thereby as an instrument of propaganda or oppression, particularly against dissenters.**

We believe in the right to universal education. Everyone has a right to the cultural opportunity to fulfill his or her unique capacities and talents. The schools should foster satisfying and productive living. They should be open at all levels to any and all; the achievement of excellence should be encouraged. **Innovative and experimental forms of education are to be welcomed.** The energy and idealism of the young deserve to be appreciated and channeled to constructive purposes.

World Community

We deplore the division of humankind on nationalistic grounds. We have reached a turning point in human history where the best option is to transcend the limits of national sovereignty and to move toward the building of a world community in which all sectors of the human family can participate. Thus we look to the development of a system of world law and a world order based upon transnational federal government.

This world community must renounce the resort to violence and force as a method of solving international disputes. We believe in the peaceful adjudication of differences by international courts and by the development of the arts of negotiation and compromise. **War is obsolete.** So is the use of nuclear, biological, and chemical weapons. It is a planetary imperative to reduce the level of military expenditures and turn these savings to peaceful and people-oriented uses.
The world community must engage in cooperative planning concerning the use of rapidly depleting resources. The planet earth must be considered a single ecosystem. **Ecological damage, resource depletion, and excessive population growth must be checked by international concord.**

The problems of economic growth and development can no longer be resolved by one nation alone; they are worldwide in scope. **It is the moral obligation of the developed nations to provide — through an international authority that safeguards human rights — massive technical, agricultural, medical, and economic assistance, including birth control techniques, to the developing portions of the globe. World poverty must cease. Hence extreme disproportions in wealth, income, and economic growth should be reduced on a worldwide basis.**

We must expand communication and transportation across frontiers. **Travel restrictions must cease**. The world must be open to diverse political, ideological, and moral viewpoints **and evolve a worldwide system of television and radio for information and education.** We thus call for full international cooperation in culture, science, the arts, and technology across ideological borders. We must learn to live openly together or we shall perish together.

Humanity As a Whole

IN CLOSING: The world cannot wait for a reconciliation of competing political or economic systems to solve its problems. These are the times for men and women of goodwill to further the building of a peaceful and prosperous world. **We urge that parochial loyalties and inflexible moral and religious ideologies be transcended.** We urge recognition of the common humanity of all people. We further urge the use of reason and compassion **to produce the kind of world we want** — a world in which peace, prosperity, freedom, and happiness are widely shared. …**The true revolution is occurring and can continue in countless nonviolent adjustments.** But this entails the willingness to step forward onto new and expanding plateaus. At the present juncture of history, **commitment to all humankind is the highest commitment of which we are capable; it transcends the narrow allegiances of church, state, party, class, or race in moving toward a wider vision of human potentiality.** What more daring a goal for humankind than for each person to become, in ideal as well as practice, a citizen of a world community. It is a classical vision; we can now give it new vitality. Humanism thus interpreted is a moral force that has time on its side. We believe that humankind has the potential, intelligence, goodwill, and cooperative skill to implement this commitment in the decades ahead.

All three of the humanist manifestos are explicitly hostile to Christianity and from them we conclude that humanism is atheistic, man-centered, and socialistic. By their own admission, there must be a "separation of ideology and state." If that is the case, then separation of school and state is an imperative, because education cannot be separated from ideology. If secular humanists are so quick to realize that Christianity is a major threat to their worldview, then why is it that Christians are so apathetic about having their children indoctrinated in the humanist worldview? Christians should be campaigning for the separation of school and state. Humanists believe in evolution, moral relativism, global government, and toleration. They promote sexual freedom, abortion, and the right to die by euthanasia or suicide. Underlying all these beliefs is intense hatred for God coupled with the desire to steal our children from us by "countless nonviolent adjustments," most of which occur in classrooms all across the country. Unfortunately, these manifestos hold within them the beliefs of the majority of Americans today. First John 4:1-6 says,

> Dear friends, do not believe every spirit, but test the spirits to see whether they are from God, because many false prophets have gone out into the world. This is how you can recognize the Spirit of God: Every spirit that acknowledges that Jesus Christ has come in the flesh is from God, *but every spirit that does not acknowledge Jesus is not from God. This is the spirit of the antichrist, which you have heard is coming and even now is already in the world.* You, dear children are from God and have overcome them, because the one who is in you is greater than the one who is in the world. They are from the world and therefore speak from the viewpoint of the world, and the world listens to them. We are from God, and whoever knows God listens to us; but whoever is not from God does not listen to us. This is how we recognize the Spirit of truth and the spirit of falsehood.

Underlying all humanist doctrine is the insidious and pernicious lie that man is basically good, that man can be perfected, that if we band together we can achieve Utopia on earth—without God. We are at the crossroads of Babel once again and the voice of defiance cries out for a new tower that reaches to the heavens. There can be no doubt that humanism in all of its forms is the voice of the anti-Christ. Our great archenemy, Satan, stands behind every humanist doctrine from the beginning of time. Humanist doctrine is quietly embedded in virtually every public school curriculum from kindergarten upwards.[16] In a speech on November 6, 1933, Hitler stated, "When an opponent declares, 'I will not come over to your side,' I calmly say, 'Your child belongs to us already…What are you? You will pass on.'"[17] Secular humanists say the same.

Soli Deo Gloria

FURTHER UP
AND
FURTHER IN

WEEK TWO—DAY ONE

Worldly Wisdom

KNOWLEDGE:

Genesis 2:8-9

Now the LORD God had planted a garden in the east, in Eden; and there he put the man he had formed. And the LORD God made all kinds of trees grow out of the ground—trees that were pleasing to the eye and good for food. In the middle of the garden were the tree of life and the tree of the knowledge of good and evil.

Genesis 2:15-17

The LORD God took the man and put him in the Garden of Eden to work it and take care of it. And the LORD God commanded the man, "You are free to eat from any tree in the garden; but you must not eat from the tree of the knowledge of good and evil, for when you eat of it you will surely die."

Genesis 3:1-7

Now the serpent was more crafty than any of the wild animals the LORD God had made. He said to the woman, "Did God really say, 'You must not eat from any tree in the garden'?"

The woman said to the serpent, "We may eat fruit from the trees in the garden, but God did say, 'You must not eat fruit from the tree that is in the middle of the garden, and you must not touch it, or you will die.'"

"You will not surely die," the serpent said to the woman. "For God knows that when you eat of it your eyes will be opened, and you will be like God, knowing good and evil."

When the woman saw that the fruit of the tree was good for food and pleasing to the eye, and also desirable for gaining wisdom, she took some and ate it. She also gave some to her husband, who was with her, and he ate it. Then the eyes of both of them were opened, and they realized they were naked; so they sewed fig leaves together and made coverings for themselves.

UNDERSTANDING:

1. What (or who) is the source of worldly wisdom?
2. How did the serpent twist God's words when he first approached Eve?
3. How did Eve add to God's words?

WISDOM:

How does the serpent's proposal exemplify the attitude expressed in the Humanist Manifesto 2: "People are more important than decalogues, rules, proscriptions, or regulations"?

NOTES

_____

_____

_____

_____

_____

_____

_____

_____

_____

_____

_____

_____

_____

_____

WEEK TWO—DAY TWO

The Tower of Babel

KNOWLEDGE:

Genesis 1:28

God blessed them and said to them, "Be fruitful and increase in number; fill the earth and subdue it. Rule over the fish of the sea and the birds of the air and over every living creature that moves on the ground."

Genesis 11:1-8

Now the whole world had one language and a common speech. As men moved eastward, they found a plain in Shinar and settled there.

They said to each other, "Come, let's make bricks and bake them thoroughly." They used brick instead of stone, and tar for mortar. Then they said, "Come, let us build ourselves a city, with a tower that reaches to the heavens, so that we may make a name for ourselves and not be scattered over the face of the whole earth."

But the LORD came down to see the city and the tower that the men were building. The LORD said, "If as one people speaking the same language they have begun to do this, then nothing they plan to do will be impossible for them. Come, let us go down and confuse their language so they will not understand each other."

So the LORD scattered them from there over all the earth, and they stopped building the city. That is why it was called Babel—because there the LORD confused the language of the whole world. From there the LORD scattered them over the face of the whole earth.

UNDERSTANDING:

1. What was God's command in Genesis 1:28?
2. How did men deliberately defy God's command?
3. What is the significance of making a name for themselves?

WISDOM:

1. Compare the people of Genesis 11 with modern-day secular humanists:

    "We deplore the division of humankind on nationalistic grounds. We have reached a turning point in human history where the best option is to transcend the limits of national sovereignty and to move toward the building of a world community in which all sectors of the human family can participate. Thus we look to the development of a system of world law and a world order based upon transnational federal government...commitment to all humankind is the highest commitment of which we are capable; it transcends the narrow allegiances of church, state, party, class, or race in moving toward a wider vision of human potentiality." —Humanist Manifesto 2

2. Consensus, group-think, and cooperation are the underpinnings of modern secular education. How do these goals support the vision of secular humanists and at the same time undermine the biblical admonition to be discerning?

NOTES

_____

_____

_____

_____

_____

_____

_____

_____

_____

_____

_____

_____

_____

Week Two—Day Three

Fools

KNOWLEDGE:

Psalm 14:1

The fool says in his heart, "There is no God."

Proverbs 1:7

The fear of the LORD is the beginning of knowledge, but fools despise wisdom and discipline.

Proverbs 1:22

How long will you simple ones love your simple ways? How long will mockers delight in mockery and fools hate knowledge?

1 Corinthians 1: 20, 25

Where is the wise man? Where is the scholar? Where is the philosopher of this age? Has not God made foolish the wisdom of the world? ...For the foolishness of God is wiser than man's wisdom, and the weakness of God is stronger than man's strength.

Romans 1:18-23, 28

The wrath of God is being revealed from heaven against all the godlessness and wickedness of men who suppress the truth by their wickedness, since what may be known about God is plain to them, because God has made it plain to them. For since the creation of the world God's invisible qualities—his eternal power and divine nature—have been clearly seen, being understood from what has been made, so that men are without excuse. For although they knew God, they neither glorified him as God nor gave thanks to him, but their thinking became futile and their foolish hearts were darkened. Although they claimed to be wise, they became fools and exchanged the glory of the immortal God for images made to look like mortal man and birds and animals and reptiles…Furthermore, since they did not think it worthwhile to retain the knowledge of God, he gave them over to a depraved mind, to do what ought not to be done.

Proverbs 3:5-7

Trust in the LORD with all your heart and lean not on your own understanding; in all your ways acknowledge him, and he will make your paths straight. Do not be wise in your own eyes; fear the LORD and shun evil.

UNDERSTANDING:

1. What does God call those who embrace secular philosophy?
2. How serious is this according to Romans 1?
3. According to the Humanist Manifesto 2, there is "insufficient evidence for belief in the existence of a supernatural." Is this true according to Romans 1?

WISDOM:

1. Many secular humanists are really nice people and make good neighbors. How do the scriptural descriptions of secular humanists fit with your personal perception of them?
2. Is your perception based on personal experience or on what the Bible says? How does Proverbs 3 address this?
3. How can our personal experiences blind us to the truth?

NOTES

WEEK TWO—DAY FOUR

The Ways of the Nations

KNOWLEDGE:

Deuteronomy 11:16-17

Be careful, or you will be enticed to turn away and worship other gods and bow down to them. Then the LORD's anger will burn against you, and he will shut the heavens so that it will not rain and the ground will yield no produce, and you will soon perish from the good land the LORD is giving you.

Deuteronomy 18:9

When you enter the land the LORD your God is giving you, do not learn to imitate the detestable ways of the nations there.

Jeremiah 10:2

This is what the LORD says:
> "Do not learn the ways of the nations
> or be terrified by signs in the sky,
> though the nations are terrified by them."

Colossians 2:2-4, 8

My purpose is that they may be encouraged in heart and united in love, so that they may have the full riches of complete understanding, in order that they may know the mystery of God, namely, Christ, in whom are hidden all the treasures of wisdom and knowledge. I tell you this so that no one may deceive you by fine-sounding arguments. See to it that no one takes you captive through hollow and deceptive philosophy, which depends on human tradition and the basic principles of this world rather than on Christ.

Colossians 2:20-22

Since you died with Christ to the basic principles of this world, why, as though you still belonged to it, do you submit to its rules: "Do not handle! Do not taste! Do not touch!"? These are all destined to perish with use, because they are based on human commands and teachings.

John 18:37

"You are a king, then!" said Pilate.
Jesus answered, "You are right in saying I am a king. In fact, for this reason I was born, and for this I came into the world, to testify to the truth. Everyone on the side of truth listens to me."

2 Thessalonians 2:13

But we ought always to thank God for you, brothers loved by the Lord, because from the beginning God chose you to be saved through the sanctifying work of the Spirit and through belief in the truth.

UNDERSTANDING:

1. The Bible is full of warnings about learning the ways of the nations and living by the principles of this world. What is the inherent danger?
2. According to Jesus, why was he born?
3. How are we saved according to 2 Thessalonians 2:13?

WISDOM:

Most Christians would heartily agree that it would be wrong to send their children to a school where they would be indoctrinated in a false religion such as Islam or Hinduism, yet they have no problem with secular humanism because there is the illusion of religious neutrality. How does that make secular humanism even more dangerous?

NOTES

_____

_____

_____

_____

_____

_____

_____

_____

_____

_____

_____

_____

_____

_____

_____

WEEK TWO—DAY FIVE

Choosing Sides

KNOWLEDGE:

John 18:37

"You are a king, then!" said Pilate. Jesus answered, "You are right in saying I am a king. In fact, for this reason I was born, and for this I came into the world, to testify to the truth. Everyone on the side of truth listens to me."

Matthew 12:30

He who is not with me is against me, and he who does not gather with me scatters.

1 John 4:1-6

Dear friends, do not believe every spirit, but test the spirits to see whether they are from God, because many false prophets have gone out into the world. This is how you can recognize the Spirit of God: Every spirit that acknowledges that Jesus Christ has come in the flesh is from God, but every spirit that does not acknowledge Jesus is not from God. This is the spirit of the antichrist, which you have heard is coming and even now is already in the world. You, dear children are from God and have overcome them, because the one who is in you is greater than the one who is in the world. They are from the world and therefore speak from the viewpoint of the world, and the world listens to them. We are from God, and whoever knows God listens to us; but whoever is not from God does not listen to us. This is how we recognize the Spirit of truth and the spirit of falsehood.

Judges 2:2

You shall not make a covenant with the people of this land, but you shall break down their altars.

UNDERSTANDING:

1. According to these verses, is it possible to be philosophically neutral?
2. On which side does secular humanism fall?

WISDOM

1. Should Christians respect the religious views of those who are not Christians? Should we agree to "live and let live" according to Judges 2:2?
2. Why was it so important that the Israelites break down the altars of pagan worship, and how should we apply that principle in our society?
3. Should Christians attend diversity training at their places of employment?
4. How much of your viewpoint is determined by what it means to be a good American citizen rather than by what Scripture teaches?

NOTES

_____

_____

_____

_____

_____

_____

_____

_____

_____

_____

_____

_____

_____

Chapter 3

Not by Default
But by Design

Part One: Primary Players in Shaping
Our Educational System

Be self-controlled and alert. Your enemy the devil prowls around
like a roaring lion looking for someone to devour.

—1 Peter 5:8

SOME CALL IT a conspiracy. Others refuse to see it at all. The fact
remains that secular humanism, an anti-Christian persuasion, is
taught in the public schools of America. Once we are familiar with its
tenets we can see evidence of it in almost every textbook. The question
we must answer is, "Did this happen by default or by design?" If the
current curriculum is merely a product of cultural drift, then the situation
is easily rectified. We simply redesign the curriculum to get us back on
track. On the other hand, if the curriculum is designed with the intent
of eradicating Christianity, then we have to conclude that the State has
declared war against the Church, and we must prepare for battle. The
point of this chapter is to prove that secular humanists have an agenda
to use education to proselytize our children, in effect luring them away
from the knowledge of God.

   In the cosmic battle, part of Satan's strategy has always been to
go after the children. Solomon recognized this when he wrote the

Two Trees of Knowledge

book of Proverbs. In Proverbs chapter nine, he describes the battle as a competition between personified Wisdom and the woman Folly, who is but another disguise of Satan. Listen to what Solomon says:

1 Wisdom has built her house;
　　she has hewn out its seven pillars.

2 She has prepared her meat and mixed her wine;
　　she has also set her table.

3 She has sent out her maids, and she calls
　　from the highest point of the city.

4 "Let all who are simple come in here!"
　　she says to those who lack judgment.

5 "Come, eat my food
　　and drink the wine I have mixed.

6 Leave your simple ways and you will live;
　　walk in the way of understanding…"

13 The woman Folly is loud;
　　she is undisciplined and without knowledge.

14 She sits at the door of her house,
　　on a seat at the highest point of the city,

15 calling out to those who pass by,
　　who go straight on their way.

16 "Let all who are simple come in here!"
　　she says to those who lack judgment.

17 "Stolen water is sweet;
　　food eaten in secret is delicious!"

18 But little do they know that the dead are there,
　　that her guests are in the depths of the grave.

Wisdom and Folly are both calling out to children, probably young adolescents. They both offer food and drink. Wisdom leads to life, and the woman Folly leads to death. The children are the trophies. The woman Folly has an agenda to steal the hearts of the children of God just as secular humanists do today. Dr. James Dobson iterates this in *Children At Risk:*

> Some will scoff at the suggestion that there is a coordinated, well thought-out strategy to win this Civil War of Values. They might suggest that we are merely witnessing a casual and random drift of social mores, shifting over time from one end of the political spectrum to the other. I wish this were true, but it is not.

> Secular humanists, particularly the more radical activists, have a specific objective in mind for the future. They hope to accomplish that goal primarily by isolating children from their parents, and they did so effectively with the parental consent issue. It will then be relatively easy to "reorient" and indoctrinate the next generation of Americans. This strategy explains why their most bitter campaigns are being waged over school curricula and other issues that involve our kids. Children are *the key* to the future.

> ...The campaign to isolate children from their parents and to indoctrinate them with humanistic ideas is being waged primarily in the public schools...[18]

This agenda is not technically a conspiracy. If it were, it would be difficult to prove this point. The truth is, anyone willing to do the research can find mountains of evidence to support the fact that there is an aggressive agenda in play. Educators depend on the fact that the majority of parents will never open their children's textbooks. They are right. Most parents trust the schools implicitly and never give the curriculum a second thought. Most parents spend more time checking out their children's babysitters than their children's teachers and textbooks.

Part of the reason parents are so willing to entrust their children to the State is that they never look beyond the nice teacher in the classroom. She may be young and pretty and love children. Or she may be older—a grandmother surrogate. She is genuinely nice and would honestly never do anything to harm a child. But what does she believe? Does she believe that all people are basically good? Does she try to build up a child's self-esteem without any reference to God? Does she believe there is absolute truth? She has been trained by the State to teach what the State mandates. That is the point of certification. Is she bucking the system, flying under the radar to be salt and light in a dark world? Or is she trying to keep her job because she has kids of her own to support? *Does she even know the difference?*

Another reason we trust the State schools is because they are located right in the middle of our neighborhoods. We know all the kids who go there, as well as most of their parents. They seem like nice people. The illusion this creates is that the school is as safe as our own backyard. This is a powerful illusion. The fact that most of us don't know what our neighbors believe doesn't faze us. We think we have control, but our kids are out of our sight for eight hours a day. What are they learning in those eight hours and what is the agenda of the educators?

Several books are available on the topic of the history of public education in America, some with Christian bias and some without. Both sources are invaluable for our purposes, and for anyone who wants a more comprehensive history, these sources are listed in the endnotes.[19] For our purposes, a condensed synopsis of people, events, and publications highlighting the humanist agenda will suffice.

Rousseau, Jean-Jacques (1712-1788). Rousseau, whose Enlightenment ideas profoundly influenced the French Revolution, had an equally profound effect on education. In fact, in the generations following his death, those who were attracted to his humanist foundations built a whole philosophy of education on his ideas. *Foundational to Rousseau's beliefs is the premise that man is essentially good, and that evil must come from without.* For Rousseau and other humanists, the origin of evil resides in social structures. Rousseau believed that since the child was born good, the best way to educate him would be to allow the natural impulses of the child to direct his learning, both what he learns and when he learns. Books were considered to be corrupting influences of society, so education would best be achieved by drawing out the natural goodness of the child, according to Rousseau.

Interestingly, Rousseau abandoned all five of his own children as infants at the Paris *Hopital des Enfants-Trouves,* so he never had the opportunity to experience this natural goodness and ease of parenting himself. He did, however, write a novel that changed the way educators have approached education ever since. The novel is *Emile*, a story about the total transformation of a ten-year-old boy in the power of a creepy teacher whose agenda is mind-control. As we learn from the tutor in asides to the reader, the tutor is programming Emile without the boy's knowledge, making the child entirely dependent on him by trifling rewards and punishments, such as a barely perceptible change in vocal tone. The child's entire education is a subtle form of invisible mind control. The effect of *Emile* on educators was far-reaching. For the first time, those in control began to see children as human resources who could be turned into assets for big business or the State. *The goals for children in Rousseau's plan were resignation and passivity, readiness to be of service for the elite.* These goals were no doubt harder to achieve without the use of Ritalin.

Pestalozzi, Johann Heinrich (1746-1827). Pestalozzi was a Swiss educational reformer who used Rousseau's ideas and implemented them in his school at Yverdon. He believed children should learn through activities rather than words and reading, hence his reputation as the inventor of multicultural fun-and-games psychological elementary schooling. Because of his firm belief in the goodness of humanity, he deplored strict discipline and sought to develop the goodness of children by showering them with affection. He believed that the natural inclinations of children should determine the learning process, not artificial teaching methods or concerns about "correctness." *As a humanist, Pestalozzi was committed to social justice and believed education was central to improving social conditions.* His most famous work was *How Gertrude Teaches Her Children* (1801). The term "social justice" applies specifically to values inherent in socialism.

Hegel, Georg Wilhelm Friedrich (1770-1831). Hegel was a Prussian philosopher who believed that the State is God. He wrote, "The Universal is to be found in the State…The State is the Divine Idea as it exists on earth…We must therefore worship the State as the manifestation of the Divine on earth, and consider that, if it is difficult to comprehend Nature, it is harder to grasp the essence of the State… the State is the march of God through the world."[20]

Hegel believed the State had supremacy over the individual and therefore the individual was to be sacrificed for the State whenever the State deemed it necessary. Hegel developed what came to be known as the Hegelian Dialectic, a psychological system of thought reform and mind control that was used on American POWs during the Korean War. In fact, this is where the term "brainwashing" originated. Hegel declared that absolute truth does not exist, but new truths are constantly being formed out of previous competing truths. In this way, truth "evolves." The dialectic is a tool to move people away from belief in absolutes, and toward "group consensus." This is the tool Stalin used

> *Let our pupil be taught that he does not belong to himself, but that he is public property.*
>
> —Benjamin Rush

to justify the murder of millions of people. Today, the Hegelian Dialectic is known by terms such as values clarification, outcome-based education, critical thinking, synthesis, dialoguing to consensus, decision-making, and a host of other names. It is used in every public school classroom in America. (More about this in chapter 7.)

Froebel, Friedrich Wilhelm August (1782-1852). Froebel was a German educator who early in life had a love of nature and became the apprentice to a forester. Later, he went to Switzerland and worked with Pestalozzi, furthering the development of his mentor's ideas. His view of children was almost idolatrous; he saw them as delicate little flowers that must be carefully tended. He is known as the inventor of kindergarten—literally a "garden of children." The teacher was merely the gardener tending to every need of the child. The whole emphasis of this education was to give the children the freedom to play and grow as freely as plants. Group activities were stressed so the child could develop *important habits of cooperation.* In the beginning, children who attended kindergartens caused problems for the teachers of elementary grades. Articles were written criticizing kindergartens for producing children who were unruly, disobedient, dependent, and continually expecting to be amused. In the end, Froebel's philosophy has not only prevailed, but has come to dominate public education at all levels, not just kindergarten.

Mann, Horace (1796-1859). Horace Mann is known as the father of American public education. In 1837 he was appointed head of the board of education in Massachusetts. His reforms included establishing a single state school system rather than having schools run by local school districts. He promoted longer school years and higher teacher pay. In 1852

> *We who are engaged in the sacred cause of education are entitled to look upon all parents as having given hostages to our cause.*
>
> *—Horace Mann*

he supported governor Edward Everett in the decision to adopt the Prussian education system in American public schools. (The Prussian system was designed to indoctrinate the citizens of Prussia, a German military state, with principles that demanded obedience to the state first and foremost. The Prussian schools imposed an official language to instill loyalty to the Crown and train young men for the military. As the German philosopher Johann Gottlieb Fichte said, "The schools must fashion the person, and fashion him in such a way that he simply cannot will otherwise than what you wish him to will." In 1763, Frederick 2 made schooling compulsory for ages five through thirteen. A centralized uniform system was implemented in 1794 under the Prussian General Land Law whereby all schools and universities were made institutions of the state. In 1810, Prussia made teacher certification and student testing mandatory.) After Massachusetts adopted the Prussian system, New York followed suit. Today, all American public education is Prussian-based.

Harris, William Torrey. U.S. Commissioner of Education from 1889 to 1906. Harris was a leading scholar of German philosophy who both standardized and Germanized our schools. He trained a generation of American intellectuals in the ideas of Prussian philosophers Kant and Hegel. He believed that children were *property* and that the state had a compelling interest in disposing of them as it pleased. Harris is the man who gave America scientifically age-graded classrooms to replace the successful mixed-age school practice. This had the effect of not only separating children from parents all day long, but now from siblings as well. The psychological impact of isolating children from all family members for eight hours a day was profound. Whereas before, children bonded primarily with parents and siblings, they now bonded with peers who became the new family. Prior to this, the phenomenon of "peer pressure" during the teen years was virtually nonexistent. Today it is still virtually nonexistent with homeschoolers.

Dewey, John (1859-1952). John Dewey was the father of progressive education, honorary president of the National Education Association in 1932, and co-author of the 1933 Humanist Manifesto.

He was a long-term member of the American Federation of Teachers, and is often cited as having provided the groundwork for outcomes-based education. Dewey wrote a theory of education and democracy that was evolution-based. He wrote in *The School and Society*, "The changes in the moral school atmosphere...are not mere accidents, they are necessities of the larger social evolution."[21] Dewey was defiantly atheistic. He wrote in *Teacher Magazine*, "There is no God and there is no soul. Hence, there are no needs

> *The children who know how to think for themselves spoil the harmony of the collective society which is coming, where everyone would be interdependent.*
>
> *—John Dewey*

for the props of traditional religion. With dogma and creed excluded, the immutable truth is also dead and buried. There is no room for fixed, natural laws or moral absolutes."[22] Dewey was also a hardcore socialist who was deeply committed to the goal of collectivizing the United States. He belonged to several socialist organizations and was president of the League for Industrial Democracy whose purpose was "education for a new social order based on production for use and not for profit." Dewey spent time in China during the 1920's and was one of dozens of progressive educators who studied in Russia in the early 1930's, returning with nothing but praise for Marx, Lenin, and Stalin. These educators were determined to impose the Russian model on American people.

In an interview on the radio talk show *Point of View*, Dr. Samuel Blumenfeld, writer of several books on American education, including *N.E.A. Trojan Horse in American Education*, charged John Dewey with being the first one to formulate the notion that high literacy rates were an obstacle to socialism.[23] High literacy rates give the individual the means to seek knowledge independently. This runs counter to the best interests of the state. There is a motive behind the "dumbing down of America." It is no accident.

Goddard, Henry H. (1866-1957). Henry Goddard was head of the Psychology Department at Princeton. He was a Darwinian racist and eugenicist who researched "feeblemindedness" and coined the term "moron." He devised intelligence tests that were designed to keep "feebleminded" immigrants from coming to America, forcing 80% of them to be deported back to their homelands. His contribution to American schooling was standardized testing which he said would make the lower classes recognize their own inferiority. His books were best sellers in Nazi Germany during the Third Reich.

Cubberly, Ellwood, P. (1868-1941). Cubberly was the dean of Stanford University's School of Education and a member of the Cleveland Group, which was an Educational Trust dedicated to a reorganization of the materials of instruction in schools of all grades. This was also the beginning of a plan to use the credentialing process to control education. Cubberly stated, "Each year the child is coming to belong more and more to the State and less to the parent."[24] He viewed education as an instrument to social engineering.

> *Only a system of state-controlled schools can be free to teach whatever the welfare of the state may demand.*
>
> *—Ellwood Cubberly*

Gramski, Antonio (1891-1937). Antonio Gramski was the founder of the Italian Communist Party who collaborated with Soviet communists to devise a strategy for conquering the West. In visits with Lenin and Stalin, he told them that they were going about conquering the West in the wrong way, that a physical battle would never deter us. Why? Because our Christianity stood in the way. He advised them to take another approach which, although it would take longer, would in the end bring victory. He advised them to deconstruct our culture, which would have two phases: 1) Delete the memory of God from every sphere of public life in America, and 2) Indoctrinate the masses with Marxist propaganda through the public education system.

In case you are tempted to laugh this off as some harebrained conspiracy theory, check out this excerpt from a ninth grade World History book that is used in American schools today:[25]

> In the economy that developed from the Industrial Revolution, a few people became enormously rich. Most, however, remained poor, including the workers whose labor drove the economy. This uneven distribution of wealth disturbed many people. Some reformers became convinced that laissez-faire capitalism was not the best economic system. They argued that laws could not do enough to remedy inequalities. The only way to distribute wealth more evenly, they felt was to change the ownership and operation of the means of production....Some of these reformers advocated a political and economic system called socialism. Under socialism, governments own the means of production and operate them for the benefit of all people, rich or poor...These reformers, called socialists, wanted to establish an economic system that would do away with the profit motive and competition. They believed everyone, not just capitalists and factory owners, had a right to share in the profits.

> Marxist Socialists often believed that violent revolution was required to get rid of capitalism. They believed this was probably the only way to establish governments that owned the means of production and controlled all economic planning...Another group of socialists, though influenced by Marx, believe that socialism could develop gradually through education...that when enough people became educated about socialism, they would elect socialist representatives to their government. Then government would take over the means of production peacefully. Owners would be paid for their property and government would operate the means of production in the interests of all people.

This same textbook has a total of three sentences about George Washington, but spends four pages on Karl Marx and Marxism. The book takes a bombastic anti-capitalist approach, teaching that in capitalism only a few have the opportunity for wealth, whereas in socialism, the wealth is shared by everyone. What typical ninth grader wouldn't be convinced?

B.F. Skinner (1904-1990). B.F. Skinner was without a doubt one of the most influential behavioral scientists of all time. In 1947 he gave the William James Lectures at Harvard University and was invited to join the Psychology Department in 1948. He is best known for his book *Walden 2*, which reveals his vision of Utopia and describes a society in which infants spend their first year of life in a sterile cubicle, and children are raised by the State rather than by their parents. The goal of behaviorists is the prediction and control of behavior. Skinner and his disciples have had a profound impact on how children are educated today. His "operant conditioning" methods are used in classrooms across the country.

Behavioral scientists continue to have a profound impact on education. One of their most important roles is designing the methods by which the curriculum is taught. This will be covered in greater detail in the chapter on deception. For now we will continue to make the case that we are where we are in education by design. The next chapter will focus on publications and bring us up to date on the current trends in education.

Soli Deo Gloria

FURTHER UP
AND
FURTHER IN

Two Trees of Knowledge

Week Three—Day One

Schemes and Conspiracies

KNOWLEDGE:

Genesis 3:1

Now the serpent was more crafty than any of the wild animals the LORD God had made. He said to the woman, "Did God really say, 'You must not eat from any tree in the garden'?"

Job 1:9-12

"Does Job fear God for nothing?" Satan replied. "Have you not put a hedge around him and his household and everything he has? You have blessed the work of his hands, so that his flocks and herds are spread throughout the land. But stretch out your hand and strike everything he has, and he will surely curse you to your face." The LORD said to Satan, "Very well, then, everything he has is in your hands, but on the man himself do not lay a finger." Then Satan went out from the presence of the LORD.

Luke 22:31

"Simon, Simon, Satan has asked to sift you as wheat…"

1 Peter 5:8

Be self-controlled and alert. Your enemy the devil prowls around like a roaring lion looking for someone to devour.

Ephesians 6:10-18

Finally, be strong in the Lord and in his mighty power. Put on the full armor of God so that you can take your stand against the devil's schemes. For our struggle is not against flesh and blood, but against the rulers, against the authorities, against the powers of this dark world and against the spiritual forces of evil in the heavenly realms. Therefore put on the full armor of God, so that when the day of evil comes, you may be able to stand your ground, and after you have done everything, to stand. Stand firm then, with the belt of truth buckled around your waist, with the breastplate of righteousness in place, and with your feet fitted with the readiness that comes from the gospel of peace. In addition to all this, take up the shield of faith, with which you can extinguish all the flaming arrows of the evil one. Take the helmet of salvation and the sword of the Spirit, which is the word of God. And pray in the Spirit on all occasions with all kinds of prayers and requests. With this in mind, be alert and always keep on praying for all the saints.

UNDERSTANDING:

1. What do we learn about Satan from these verses? Does he plan ahead or merely commit random acts of assault?
2. Can Satan do anything without God's permission?
3. Does God sometimes give him permission to assault those God loves?

WISDOM:

Is it out of the question to believe that there is a present-day conspiracy against Christians?

NOTES

_____

_____

_____

_____

_____

_____

_____

_____

_____

_____

_____

_____

_____

WEEK THREE—DAY TWO

Total Depravity

The Calvinistic term "total depravity" has been misunderstood by many Christians to mean something akin to "utter depravity." This is not the biblical view. By "total depravity" we simply mean that every part of man's nature was corrupted by the fall—not only his flesh, but his heart, his mind, and his will. With this in mind, study the following verses.

KNOWLEDGE:

Genesis 6:5

The LORD saw how great man's wickedness on the earth had become, and that every inclination of the thoughts of his heart was only evil all the time.

Jeremiah 17:9

The heart is deceitful above all things and beyond cure. Who can understand it?

Romans 8:7-8

The sinful mind is hostile to God. It does not submit to God's law, nor can it do so. Those controlled by the sinful nature cannot please God.

Ephesians 4:17-19

So I tell you this, and insist on it in the Lord, that you must no longer live as the Gentiles do, in the futility of their thinking. They are darkened in their understanding and separated from the life of God because of the ignorance that is in them due to the hardening of their hearts. Having lost all sensitivity, they have given themselves over to sensuality so as to indulge in every kind of impurity, with a continual lust for more.

Titus 1:15

To the pure, all things are pure, but to those who are corrupted and do not believe, nothing is pure. In fact, both their minds and consciences are corrupted.

John 8:44 (ESV)

You are of your father the devil, and your will is to do your father's desires. He was a murderer from the beginning, and has nothing to do with the truth, because there is no truth in him. When he lies, he speaks out of his own character, for he is a liar and the father of lies.

Isaiah 5:20

Woe to those who call evil good and good evil, who put darkness for light and light for darkness, who put bitter for sweet and sweet for bitter.

UNDERSTANDING:

1. How do these verses show that every part of man's nature was corrupted by the fall?
2. How does this biblical doctrine compare with the humanist doctrine espoused by Rousseau, Hegel, Dewey, and others?

WISDOM:

Explain why belief in the goodness of man is so dangerous.

NOTES

WEEK THREE—DAY THREE

Discernment

KNOWLEDGE:

1 Kings 3:9-12

"So give your servant a discerning heart to govern your people and to distinguish between right and wrong. For who is able to govern this great people of yours?" The LORD was pleased that Solomon had asked for this. So God said to him, "Since you have asked for this and not for long life or wealth for yourself, nor have asked for the death of your enemies but for discernment in administering justice, I will do what you have asked. I will give you a wise and discerning heart, so that there will never have been anyone like you, nor will there ever be."

Proverbs 3:21

My son, preserve sound judgment and discernment, do not let them out of your sight.

Psalm 119:125

I am your servant; give me discernment that I may understand your statutes.

Romans 12:2

Do not conform any longer to the pattern of this world, but be transformed by the renewing of your mind. Then you will be able to test and approve what God's will is—his good, pleasing and perfect will.

Philippians 1:10

And this is my prayer: that your love may abound more and more in knowledge and depth of insight, so that you may be able to discern what is best and may be pure and blameless until the day of Christ.

UNDERSTANDING AND WISDOM:

1. The mantra of John Dewey and modern secular humanists is "consensus." John Dewey said, "The children who know how to think for themselves spoil the harmony of the collective society which is coming." Why are citizens who are discerning such a threat to the State?

2. Cooperation and consensus are valued within the Christian community as well. Describe the difference between what Christians mean by these terms and what the educators have in mind.

NOTES

_____

_____

_____

_____

_____

_____

_____

_____

_____

_____

_____

_____

_____

WEEK THREE—DAY FOUR

Private Property

KNOWLEDGE:

Genesis 15:18

On that day the LORD made a covenant with Abram and said, "To your descendants I give this land, from the river of Egypt to the great river, the Euphrates.

Joshua 21:43

So the LORD gave Israel all the land he had sworn to give their forefathers, and they took possession of it and settled there.

1 Kings 21:1-3

Some time later there was an incident involving a vineyard belonging to Naboth the Jezreelite. The vineyard was in Jezreel, close to the palace of Ahab king of Samaria. Ahab said to Naboth, "Let me have your vineyard to use for a vegetable garden, since it is close to my palace. In exchange I will give you a better vineyard or, if you prefer, I will pay you whatever it is worth." But Naboth replied, "The LORD forbid that I should give you the inheritance of my fathers."

1 Kings 21:17-19

Then the word of the LORD came to Elijah the Tishbite: "Go down to meet Ahab king of Israel, who rules in Samaria. He is now in Naboth's vineyard, where he has gone to take possession of it. Say to him, 'This is what the LORD says: Have you not murdered a man and seized his property?' Then say to him, 'This is what the LORD says: In the place where dogs licked up Naboth's blood, dogs will lick up your blood—yes, yours!'"

Exodus 20:15

You shall not steal.

UNDERSTANDING:

1. What is the biblical stance on private property? Does God condone or forbid private ownership?
2. Do people have the right to take what belongs to someone else?
3. Study the story of Ahab and Naboth. Does the State have a right to take what belongs to someone else? Can the State steal? Can the State commit murder?

WISDOM:

1. How do the economic systems of Marxism and Communism deprive people of their God-given rights?
2. Our American government promotes massive redistribution of wealth through taxation for welfare, education, and a host of other programs. Is this stealing? Can you support your opinion from Scripture?
3. What about eminent domain?
4. To whom does the world belong, to God or to the government? To whom does our country belong?

NOTES

Historical Revisionism

KNOWLEDGE:

1 Kings 12:25-33

Then Jeroboam fortified Shechem in the hill country of Ephraim and lived there. From there he went out and built up Peniel. Jeroboam thought to himself, "The kingdom will now likely revert to the house of David. If these people go up to offer sacrifices at the temple of the LORD in Jerusalem, they will again give their allegiance to their LORD, Rehoboam king of Judah. They will kill me and return to King Rehoboam." After seeking advice, the king made two golden calves. He said to the people, "It is too much for you to go up to Jerusalem. Here are your gods, O Israel, who brought you up out of Egypt." One he set up in Bethel, and the other in Dan. And this thing became a sin; the people went even as far as Dan to worship the one there. Jeroboam built shrines on high places and appointed priests from all sorts of people, even though they were not Levites. He instituted a festival on the fifteenth day of the eighth month, like the festival held in Judah, and offered sacrifices on the altar. This he did in Bethel, sacrificing to the calves he had made. And at Bethel he also installed priests at the high places he had made. On the fifteenth day of the eighth month, a month of his own choosing, he offered sacrifices on the altar he had built at Bethel. So he instituted the festival for the Israelites and went up to the altar to make offerings.

2 Chronicles 11:5-17

Rehoboam lived in Jerusalem and built up towns for defense in Judah: Bethlehem, Etam, Tekoa, Beth Zur, Soco, Adullam, Gath, Mareshah, Ziph, Adoraim, Lachish, Azekah, Zorah, Aijalon and Hebron. These were fortified cities in Judah and Benjamin. He strengthened their defenses and put commanders in them, with supplies of food, olive oil and wine. He put shields and spears in all the cities, and made them very strong. So Judah and Benjamin were his. The priests and Levites from all their districts throughout Israel sided with him. The Levites even abandoned their pasturelands and property, and came to Judah and Jerusalem because Jeroboam and his sons had rejected them as priests of the LORD. And he appointed his own priests for the high places and for the goat and calf idols he had made. Those from every tribe of Israel who set their hearts on seeking the LORD, the God of Israel, followed the Levites to Jerusalem to offer sacrifices to the LORD, the God of their fathers. They strengthened the kingdom of Judah and supported Rehoboam son of Solomon three years, walking in the ways of David and Solomon during this time.

UNDERSTANDING AND WISDOM:

Antonio Gramski advised Lenin and Stalin to deconstruct our culture by deleting the memory of God from every sphere of public life in America and by revising history. How did Jeroboam do this very effectively in Israel?

It is interesting to note that Israel never again had a godly king. Except for a very small remnant that God saved for himself, an entire nation suffered eternal damnation because they did not know God.

Can you think of ways this is happening in our society today?

NOTES

Chapter 4

Not by Default
But by Design

Part Two: Publications and Quotes

"So I tell you this, and insist on it in the Lord, that you must no longer live as the Gentiles do, in the futility of their thinking. They are darkened in their understanding and separated from the life of God because of the ignorance that is in them due to the hardening of their hearts."

—Ephesians 4:17-18

THOSE WHO CONTROL education in our country are not really trying to disguise their goals. Their statements and publications are very clear about what they believe the purpose of education is, and about what methodologies should be employed. They are fairly certain that parents will never read these publications. In the information that they do give to parents, their stated goals are rewritten to appeal to what the parents want to hear. For example, the State takes great pains to ensure that each child will be able to choose his own values. Parents take this to mean that when a child comes to school with certain values, the school will not interfere. What it really means is that parents do not have the right to instill values into the child. At school, the child will be given choices that he would never be given at home, and he is encouraged to make his choices independently of what his parents believe. He may consult his parents, but he is strongly seduced into making choices other than the ones his parents choose.

Teachers are coming more and more to see themselves as the experts when it comes to training our children; parents are merely custodians who provide room and board for them. Parents have been strong-armed into medicating their children, enrolling them in special classes, and pushing them ahead when they should be held back. Parents who have concerns are considered to be troublemakers. In many cases, social services are called in before parents are even notified of behavioral problems. Some parents are never notified at all when their children are in counseling with State-appointed social workers. In many cases, parents have no recourse against a teacher's decision regarding the children.

It is important that parents realize that when they turn their children over to the State for education, they are voluntarily giving up their parental rights in many areas. The following quotes and publications may help parents understand just how critical this is.

1864. John Swett, California State Superintendent of Public Instruction, states, "The vulgar impression that parents have a right to dictate to teachers is entirely erroneous... If his [the teacher's] conduct is approved by his employers, the parents have no remedy against him."[26]

1919. *A Social History of the American Family* Vol. 3 by Arthur Wallace Calhoun is published. These volumes were used as social service textbooks for many years. In his third volume we read,

> The new view is that the higher and more obligatory relation is to society rather than to the family; the family goes back to the age of savagery while the State belongs to the age of civilization. The modern individual is a world citizen, served by the world, and home interests can no longer be supreme. ...The school begins to assume responsibility for the functions thrust upon it ...The kindergarten

grows downward toward the cradle and there arises talk of neighbor-hood nurseries…The child passes more and more into the custody of community experts. …We may expect in the socialist commonwealth a system of public educational agencies that will begin with the nursery and follow the individual through life.

Anyone who is keeping up with current trends in American politics will see that this is happening already. Hillary Clinton has her heart set on micro-chipping babies—for their own safety of course.

1930. The **Dick and Jane** reading series uses "whole word" and "look-say" techniques to teach reading, replacing the teaching of ABC's and phonics. It should be noted that by the end of fourth grade, phonics trained students can read an estimated 24,000 words while whole-word students have memorized only 1,600 words. Is there a conspiracy to keep literacy down, while pretending to promote literacy? Here are some things to look at: 1) At the start of World War 2, 1942-1944, the literacy rate was 96%; 2) In 1951, at the beginning of the Korean War, literacy had dropped to 81%; 3) By the end of the Vietnam War, the literacy rate was 73%. In 1993, 96.5% of the American population was mediocre to illiterate where deciphering print is concerned, according to the National Adult Literacy Survey, which represented 190 million U.S. adults over the age of 16 with an average school attendance of 12.4 years.[27]

1933. *The Great Technology* by Harold Rugg (1886-1960), author of 14 Social Studies textbooks, teachers' guides, course outlines, and student workbooks, was used by 5 million American school children in the 1930's. In this book, Rugg asserts:

A new public mind is to be created. How? Only by creating tens of millions of new individual minds and welding them into a new social mind. Old stereotypes must be broken up and new climates of opinion formed in the neighborhoods of America. But that is the task of the building of a science of society for the schools. …First, the development of a new philosophy of life and education which will be fully appropriate to the new social order; second, the building of an adequate plan for the production of a new race of educational workers; third, the making of new activities and materials for the curriculum.

Rugg was a professor of education at Teachers College, Columbia University. He trained the next generation of teachers.

1948. *UNESCO: Its Philosphy and Purpose,* **by Sir Julian Huxley** states:

The general philosophy of UNESCO (United Nations Educational Scientific and Cultural Organization) should be a scientific world humanism, global in extent and evolutionary in background…In its education program it can stress the ultimate need for world political unity and familiarize all peoples with the implication of the transfer of full sovereignty from separate nations to a world organization…to help the emergence of a single world culture."

Huxley also said, "Operationally, God is beginning to resemble not a ruler, but the last fading smile of a cosmic Cheshire Cat."

1964. Benjamin Bloom writes *Taxonomy of Educational Objectives, Handbook 2: Affective Domain* in which he states, "A large part of what we call 'good teaching' is the teacher's ability to attain affective objectives through challenging the student's fixed beliefs." He believed the purpose of education was to "change the thoughts, feelings and actions of students."

1965. The Elementary and Secondary Education Act was passed. This act was extremely important because it allowed the federal government to fund psychological and psychiatric programs in the schools. Now teachers were part of a school staff comprised of social workers, psychologists, psychiatrists, government agencies, and other specialists. The Act allows schools to do psychological testing, which they routinely do without parental consent. The only consent they need is from their team of "experts." Do they think our children are sick? Apparently so. Read on....

1973. Dr. Chester M. Pierce, a Harvard psychiatrist, gave the keynote address at the 1973 Childhood International Education Seminar in Boulder, Colorado. This is what he had to say:

> Every child entering school at the age of five is mentally ill because he comes to school with certain allegiances to our founding fathers, toward our elected officials, toward his parents, toward a belief in a supernatural being, and toward the sovereignty of this nation as a separate entity. It's up to you as teachers to make all these sick children well—by creating the international child of the future.

1973. NEA President Catherine Barrett wrote an article for the *Saturday Review of Education* in which she said,

> Dramatic changes in the way we will raise our children in the year 2000 are indicated, particularly in terms of schooling...We will need to recognize that the so-called 'basic skills' which currently represent nearly the total effort in elementary schools, will be taught in one-quarter of the present school day...When this happens—and it's near—the teacher can rise to his true calling. More than a dispenser of information, the teacher will be a conveyor of values, a philosopher... We will be agents of change.

1979. U.S. Department of Education is established. As part of a campaign promise to the NEA for supporting him, Jimmy Carter pushed hard to establish a federal department of education, despite widespread public sentiment against it.

1983. *The Humanist* includes a prize-winning essay by John Dunphy in which he says,

> I am convinced that the battle for humankind's future must be waged and won in the public school classroom by teachers that correctly perceive their role as proselytizers of a new faith…The classroom must and will become an arena of conflict between the old and the new—the rotting corpse of Christianity, together with all its adjacent evils and misery, and the new faith of humanism, resplendent with the promise of a world in which the never-realized Christian ideal of "love thy neighbor" will finally be achieved.

1989. President Bush calls an Education Summit for all fifty governors to discuss government schooling. (Bill Clinton was among those planning the six goals of America 2000.) During one presentation by Shirley McCune, Senior Director with the Mid-Continent Regional Educational Laboratory, she said,

> What's happening in America today…is a total transformation of our society. We have moved into a new era…I'm not sure we have really begun to comprehend…the incredible amount of organizational restructuring and human resource development restructuring…What we're into is the total restructuring of society.

According to John Taylor Gatto, there is no record of a single governor objecting.[28]

1990. NCEE Report—Hillary Clinton was on the board of directors of the National Center on Education and the Economy when NCEE published a report called *America's Choice: High Skills or Low Wages*. This report advocated major changes in both education and business. The thrust of the report was that by the year 2000, over 70% of the jobs in the U.S. would not require a college education. The recommendations were to reserve an elite who would attend college, but stated, "Most employees under this model need not be educated. It is far more important that they be reliable, steady, and willing to follow directions." When Bill Clinton was elected President in 1992, Marc Tucker, president of NCEE, wrote to Hillary: "…we were discussing what you and Bill should do now about education, training, and labor market policy…We think the great opportunity you have is to remold the entire American system for human resource development…"[29] The legacy left by Bill and Hillary Clinton put the control of public school curriculum in the hands of the federal government. (See 1994.)

1993. No one wants to believe that American children are victims of brainwashing and psychological conditioning. It sounds too much like a spurious conspiracy theory. But in 1993, Thomas Sowell[30] wrote *Indoctrinating the Children,* which was published in *Forbes* magazine. He wrote:

> The techniques of brainwashing developed in totalitarian countries are routinely used in psychological conditioning programs imposed on American school children. These include emotional shock and desensitization, psychological isolation from sources of support, stripping away defenses, manipulative cross-examination of the individual's underlying moral values, and inducing acceptance of alternative values by psychological rather than rational means.[31]

Recall that Wundtian Ivan Pavlov and John Dewey, two men very influential in educational circles, had strong connections to Russia and China, where psychological manipulation was deeply imbedded in school pedagogy. Russia, China, Japan, and the Pacific Islands have been practicing psychological schooling for over a century, and their techniques have now been adopted by the social engineers of the West. When we think about things like brainwashing and mind manipulation, our imaginations may take us to interrogation rooms with bright lights or sleep deprivation or other kinds of torture. However, as we know from studying the cults, all it takes to brainwash a person is a classroom and a teacher.

1994. President Bill Clinton became the answer to Marc Tucker's dreams. He saw to it that three bills were signed into law that handed control of public school curriculum to the federal government. The first of these was Goals 2000 Educate America Act, which the president himself had a hand in writing back in the 80's, and more commonly known as Goals 2000. The second was the School-to-Work Opportunities Act. This act is a variation on the former Outcome-Based Education. Outcome-Based Education was designed to train a work force specifically geared to fit the government's estimated labor needs. Under this system, the purpose of education changed from imparting academic knowledge and skills to vocational training. School-to-Work puts students in elementary grades on a track (determined by experts) that they will follow all the way to their first job. Career counselors decide each student's future career. The third law was the result of a federal appropriations bill for most federal education programs, called HR6. While it is true that the Goals 2000 law states many times over that it is voluntary, the effect of HR6 was to say that non-compliance by any state to Goals 2000 would result in that state losing all federal funding. The result of these three interconnected laws is that the federal government is now in charge of all education, including the curriculum. These laws may not have passed if written into one bill, but by parceling them out, lawmakers were deliberately deceptive.

1996. Albert Shanker, long time president of the American Federation of Teachers, in one of his last Sunday advertisements in *The New York Times,* had this to say, "Public schools do not exist to please Johnny's parents. They do not even exist to ensure that Johnny will earn a good living at a job he likes."

2001. No Child Left Behind has insured even more control by the federal government. Any state that does not adopt NCLB will lose its federal funding. All teachers are required to be state certified and licensed to assure compliance with government goals. The phrase "scientifically based research" is repeatedly found in the language of the NCLB Act. Schools are required to use "scientifically based research" in the classroom and in the development of staff. Each state is allowed to set its own achievement standards because of the provision in the tenth amendment to the U.S. Constitution that stipulates powers not granted to the federal government are reserved powers of the individual state. While this is a good thing, the result is that many states have lowered their standards in order to improve their test scores.

2006. *TOUGH CHOICES OR TOUGH TIMES* is the report of the New Commission on the Skills of the American Workforce. The summary of this report can be found on their website at www.skillscommission.org. This is part of the National Center on Education and the Economy. As you can see, the very name of this group is evidence that education is based on government projections of future workforce needs. This report is descendent from "America's Choice: High Skills or Low Wages!" written in part by Hillary Clinton. Here are some excerpts from the summary:[32]

- Our first step is creating a set of Board Examinations... **Students who score well enough will be guaranteed the right to go to their community college** to begin a program leading to a two-year technical degree or a two-year program designed to enable the student to transfer later into a four-year State college... **assuming they do well enough on their second set of Board exams, they can go off to a selective college or university.**

- Many of our teachers are superb. **But we have for a long time gotten better teachers than we deserved because of the limited opportunities for women and minorities in our workforce.** Those opportunities are far wider now, and we are left with the reality that we are now recruiting more and more of our teachers from the bottom third of the high school students going to college than is wise. To succeed, we must recruit many more from the top third.

• We would have teachers employed by the state, not the local districts, on a statewide salary schedule... The current policies regarding teacher education would be scrapped. **The state would create a new Teacher Development Agency charged with recruiting, training, and certifying teachers.** The state would launch national recruiting campaigns, **allocate slots for training the needed number of teachers**... then the task will be to **create instructional materials fashioned in the same spirit and train our teachers to use the standards, assessments, syllabi, and materials as well as possible.**

• The additional funds for serving schools with high concentrations of disadvantaged students will **make it possible for those schools to stay open from early in the morning until late at night,** offering a wide range of supportive services to the students and their families. They will have the **funds needed to screen and diagnose their students**... and the State Teacher Development Agencies will be charged with making a **special effort to recruit first-rate teachers for our minority children who look like them and can connect with these children.**

• The funds freed up by the Commission's proposals for altering the student progression through the system, will for the first time make it possible for the whole nation to do what should have been done many years ago...**provide high-quality early childhood education to its 3 and 4 year-olds.**

• The Commission proposes that **the federal government pass legislation entitling every adult and young adult worker—at no charge—to the education required** to meet the standard set by the new Board Exam standards.

- We propose that the government of the United States create Personal Competitiveness Accounts **enabling everyone to get the continuing education and training they will need throughout their work lives. The government would create these accounts for every baby when born, with an initial deposit of $500, and continue to contribute** at a lower level until that young person is 16, and later if the account holder was earning very little.

- The role of the school board would change. **Schools would no longer be owned by local school districts.** [School boards] would be responsible for connecting the schools to a wide range of social services in the community.

Public schools in the United States have always been about the economy and the workforce more than about education. Many parents have often wondered why the literacy rates in our country are staggeringly low. Here is what the educators say about it in the same summary:

> The governance, organizational, and **management scheme of American schools** was created in the early years of the 20th century to match the organization of the time. It was no doubt **appropriate for an era when most work required relatively low literacy levels…**[33]

The same people who "managed" the schools in the 20th century are managing the schools now. Why should we trust them? They are not concerned about education. They are concerned about their socially engineered Utopia. Right now we have the right to homeschool or send our children to Christian schools, but that may also come to an end. The new proposals set forth in this report seem to indicate that worldview incompatibilities may be outlawed in the future:

> A system that pursues the wrong goals more efficiently is not a system this country needs.

No organization could operate a school that was not affiliated with a helping organization of the State, unless the school was itself such an organization.[34]

If the proposals in this report ever become law, the freedoms this country was founded for will be forever gone. Equal opportunity will become a distant memory. The government will select who gets an education and who does not, and will only train a certain number of people for designated careers. There is no doubt that with secular humanism as the philosophy undergirding our educational system, the result will be a complete reformatting of the society in which we live. Without God, without the hope of heaven, the best that humankind can achieve is man-made Utopia. History has shown us that the results will be violence, corruption, ethnic cleansing, and a host of other hellish scenarios. Genesis is clear. The fruit of the tree of the knowledge of good and evil will end in death. When man without God takes it upon himself to judge what is good and what is evil, he will be deceived. Our only hope is to educate the next generation in a biblical worldview before we have that option taken from us. To do that, parents must reclaim the responsibility that God gave them in the first place.

> *I am afraid that the schools will prove the very gates of hell, unless they diligently labor in explaining the Holy Scriptures and engraving them in the heart of the youth.*
>
> *—Martin Luther*

Soli Deo Gloria

98

FURTHER UP
AND
FURTHER IN

Week Four—Day One

The Written Word

KNOWLEDGE:

Deuteronomy 28:58-59

If you do not carefully follow all the words of this law, which are written in this book, and do not revere this glorious and awesome name—the LORD your God—the LORD will send fearful plagues on you and your descendants, harsh and prolonged disasters, and severe and lingering illnesses.

Malachi 3:16

Then those who feared the LORD talked with each other, and the LORD listened and heard. A scroll of remembrance was written in his presence concerning those who feared the LORD and honored his name.

John 1:1

In the beginning was the Word, and the Word was with God, and the Word was God.

John 20:31

But these are written that you may believe that Jesus is the Christ, the Son of God, and that by believing you may have life in his name.

1 Corinthians 10:11

These things happened to them as examples and were written down as warnings for us, on whom the fulfillment of the ages has come.

UNDERSTANDING:

1. How does God communicate with men?
2. How important is it that God's people are able to read and write?

WISDOM:

The Bible is not an easy book to read. It contains words and concepts that people do not come across in ordinary reading. Many adults today are biblically illiterate due in large part to the fact that they are unable to effectively read and understand Scripture. In the summary of *Tough Choices Tough Times*, educators admit that literacy levels were kept down deliberately as part of the "management scheme of American schools." How does this effectually censor the kinds of literature people are able to read?

NOTES

_____

_____

_____

_____

_____

_____

_____

_____

_____

_____

_____

_____

_____

_____

WEEK FOUR—DAY TWO

Hating Evil

KNOWLEDGE:

Proverbs 6:16-19

There are six things the LORD hates, seven that are detestable to him: haughty eyes, a lying tongue, hands that shed innocent blood, a heart that devises wicked schemes, feet that are quick to rush into evil, a false witness who pours out lies and a man who stirs up dissension among brothers.

Psalm 5:5

The arrogant cannot stand in your presence; you hate all who do wrong.

Psalm 45:7

You love righteousness and hate wickedness; therefore God, your God, has set you above your companions by anointing you with the oil of joy.

Proverbs 8:13

To fear the LORD is to hate evil; I hate pride and arrogance, evil behavior and perverse speech.

Proverbs 13:5

The righteous hate what is false, but the wicked bring shame and disgrace.

Amos 5:15

Hate evil, love good; maintain justice in the courts.

Two Trees of Knowledge

Romans 12:9

Love must be sincere. Hate what is evil; cling to what is good.

Psalm 52:1-7

Why do you boast of evil, you mighty man?
Why do you boast all day long,
you who are a disgrace in the eyes of God?

Your tongue plots destruction;
it is like a sharpened razor,
you who practice deceit.

You love evil rather than good,
falsehood rather than speaking the truth.
Selah

You love every harmful word,
O you deceitful tongue!

Surely God will bring you down to everlasting ruin:
He will snatch you up and tear you from your tent;
he will uproot you from the land of the living.
Selah

The righteous will see and fear;
they will laugh at him, saying,

"Here now is the man
who did not make God his stronghold
but trusted in his great wealth
and grew strong by destroying others!"

UNDERSTANDING:

1. According to Proverbs 6:16-19 and Psalm 5:5, whom does God hate?
2. What are we commanded to hate?
3. How does Psalm 52 show that the wicked are at complete odds with God?

WSIDOM:

List the things in our culture that God hates and that we should hate.

NOTES

_____

_____

_____

_____

_____

_____

_____

_____

_____

_____

_____

_____

_____

_____

WEEK FOUR—DAY THREE

False Teachers

KNOWLEDGE:

Matthew 7:15-19

"Watch out for false prophets. They come to you in sheep's clothing, but inwardly they are ferocious wolves. By their fruit you will recognize them. Do people pick grapes from thornbushes, or figs from thistles? Likewise every good tree bears good fruit, but a bad tree bears bad fruit. A good tree cannot bear bad fruit, and a bad tree cannot bear good fruit. Every tree that does not bear good fruit is cut down and thrown into the fire."

Mark 8:15

"Be careful," Jesus warned them. "Watch out for the yeast of the Pharisees and that of Herod."

1 Timothy 6:3-4

If anyone teaches false doctrines and does not agree to the sound instruction of our Lord Jesus Christ and to godly teaching, he is conceited and understands nothing.

2 Peter 2:1-3;10-12

But there were also false prophets among the people, just as there will be false teachers among you. They will secretly introduce destructive heresies, even denying the sovereign Lord who bought them—bringing swift destruction on themselves. Many will follow their shameful ways and will bring the way of truth into disrepute. In their greed these teachers will exploit you with stories they have made up. Their condemnation has long been hanging over them, and their destruction has not been sleeping... Bold and arrogant, these men are not afraid to slander celestial beings; yet even angels, although they are stronger and more powerful, do not bring slanderous accusations against such beings in the presence of the Lord. But these men blaspheme in matters they do not understand. They are like brute beasts, creatures of instinct, born only to be caught and destroyed, and like beasts they too will perish.

Revelation 22:15

Outside are the dogs, those who practice magic arts, the sexually immoral, the murderers, the idolaters and everyone who loves and practices falsehood.

UNDERSTANDING:

1. What are the characteristics of false prophets and false teachers?
2. What will ultimately happen to them?

WISDOM:

During Bible times teaching took place in the churches and synagogues and in the home. That is why there are so many warnings about false teachers infiltrating the church. Jesus also warns about the false teachings of the State (Herod) in Mark 8:15. Where are the false teachers in our culture?

NOTES

_____

_____

_____

_____

_____

_____

_____

_____

_____

_____

_____

_____

_____

_____

Week Four—Day Four

Students

KNOWLEDGE:

Matthew 5:13

"You are the salt of the earth. But if the salt loses its saltiness, how can it be made salty again? It is no longer good for anything, except to be thrown out and trampled by men."

Matthew 10:24

"A student is not above his teacher, nor a servant above his master. It is enough for the student to be like his teacher, and the servant like his master."

Matthew 15:14

He replied, "Every plant that my heavenly Father has not planted will be pulled up by the roots. Leave them; they are blind guides. If a blind man leads a blind man, both will fall into a pit."

Luke 6:39-40

He also told them this parable: "Can a blind man lead a blind man? Will they not both fall into a pit? A student is not above his teacher, but everyone who is fully trained will be like his teacher."

1 Corinthians 15:33

Do not be misled: "Bad company corrupts good character." Come back to your senses as you ought, and stop sinning; for there are some who are ignorant of God—I say this to your shame.

Proverbs 4:14-19

Do not set foot on the path of the wicked or walk in the way of evil men. Avoid it, do not travel on it; turn from it and go on your way. For they cannot sleep till they do evil; they are robbed of slumber till they make someone fall. They eat the bread of wickedness and drink the wine of violence. The path of the righteous is like the first gleam of dawn, shining ever brighter till the full light of day. But the way of the wicked is like deep darkness; they do not know what makes them stumble.

Hebrews 5:13-14

Anyone who lives on milk, being still an infant, is not acquainted with the teaching about righteousness. But solid food is for the mature, who by constant use have trained themselves to distinguish good from evil.

UNDERSTANDING:

1. According to Jesus, who are students like? Why do you suppose this is true?
2. What happens to students who follow spiritually blind teachers?
3. How often does good character influence bad company?
4. Who is able to distinguish good from evil according to Hebrews 5:14?

WISDOM:

When Jesus gave his teaching about salt and light, he was speaking to his disciples (Matthew 5:1).

1. Many parents believe their children should be "salt and light" in the public schools. According to the above Scriptures, what are the chances that a spiritually immature student who is not fully equipped for spiritual battle will be successful in this endeavor?

2. What happens to salt that loses its saltiness? Part of the agenda of State schooling is to create a "global student." How would this "de-salt" a Christian student?

NOTES

_____

_____

_____

_____

_____

_____

_____

_____

_____

_____

_____

_____

_____

Week Four—Day Five

Peace

KNOWLEDGE:

Jeremiah 6:13-14

From the least to the greatest, all are greedy for gain; prophets and priests alike, all practice deceit. They dress the wound of my people as though it were not serious. "Peace, peace," they say, when there is no peace.

Ezekiel 13:10-12

Because they lead my people astray, saying, "Peace," when there is no peace, and because, when a flimsy wall is built, they cover it with whitewash, therefore tell those who cover it with whitewash that it is going to fall. Rain will come in torrents, and I will send hailstones hurtling down, and violent winds will burst forth. When the wall collapses, will people not ask you, "Where is the whitewash you covered it with?"

Matthew 10:34

Do not suppose that I have come to bring peace to the earth. I did not come to bring peace, but a sword.

John 14:27

Peace I leave with you; my peace I give you. I do not give to you as the world gives. Do not let your hearts be troubled and do not be afraid.

John 16:33

I have told you these things, so that in me you may have peace. In this world you will have trouble. But take heart! I have overcome the world.

Philippians 4:7

And the peace of God, which transcends all understanding, will guard your hearts and your minds in Christ Jesus.

UNDERSTANDING:

1. Can the world deliver any kind of peace at all?
2. What did Jesus mean when he said, "I did not come to being peace, but a sword"?
3. How is Jesus' peace radically different from world peace?
4. Will there ever be time on this present earth when there is world peace according to John 16:33?

WISDOM:

1. Secular humanism is all about world peace. That is why there is such an emphasis on consensus, cooperation, and compromise. Does Jesus ever suggest that Christians should work for world peace? Reference Matthew 10:34.
2. How are secular humanists like the false prophets mentioned in Jeremiah and Ezekiel?
3. Explain Hebrews 12:14 ("Make every effort to live in peace with all men and to be holy; without holiness no one will see the Lord.") in light of the fact that the world is always at enmity with God. What kind of peace is the author referring to—corporate peace or individual peace with one's neighbors?

NOTES

Chapter 5

Sphere Sovereignty
and the State

*The boundary lines have fallen for me in pleasant places; surely I
have a delightful inheritance.*

—Psalm 16:6

GOD CREATED MAN in his image, designing us for fellowship and community, following the pattern of fellowship and
community within the Triune Godhead. As a result, each of our social
structures bears the imprint of the Trinity. To better understand the order
within these structures, we must first look at the Trinity. Although all
the members of the Trinity are equal, there is an apparent hierarchy of
command, with God the Father at the top. Jesus, the Son, submits to
the Father. The Holy Spirit, who proceeds from the Father and the Son,
carries out the will of both Father and Son.

The social structures God has designed for us—the family, the
church, the community, the workplace, the state, and others—follow the
same pattern. For example, within the church, the chain of command
begins with Christ as the head of the church. The leaders of the church
submit to Christ, and the congregation submits to both Christ and the
leaders. Within the family, the husband is the head of the wife, and the

children submit to both husband and wife. Even the state follows this paradigm with God as the head of the state, the king in submission to God, and the citizens in submission to both God and the king.

There are several social structures, but for our purposes, we will study only the church, the family, and the State. Each social structure serves a particular purpose, and each has its own roles and responsibilities. Each structure also has boundaries that are not to be crossed. Applying the biblical principles that define these boundaries, Abraham Kuyper, (1837-1920) a Dutch theologian, journalist, and prime minister of the Netherlands, developed the concept of "sphere sovereignty." "Sphere sovereignty" suggests that each social structure is equal to the others and has been given a sovereign charge to accomplish its purpose under God. No sphere has the right to usurp the responsibilities of another sphere. For example, the church may not try to control affairs of state, nor may the state take over the responsibilities of families or the church. To do so would be a transgression against the design of God. As we will see from Scripture, God does not take these transgressions lightly.

Of all the spheres, the State is the most likely to overstep its bounds and take control of the other spheres. The Old Testament is filled with such examples. King Saul did not wait for the prophet Samuel to make sacrifices of burnt offerings, but went ahead and offered the sacrifices himself, which cost him the kingdom (1 Samuel 13:7-14). When King Jeroboam tore the ten northern tribes away from King Rehoboam, the first thing he did was get rid of all the priests and Levites in the land, so he could set up two golden calves for the people to worship. In response, God raised up another king to cut off the family of Jeroboam (1 Kings 12:25-13:10; 2 Chronicles 11:11-13). King Uzziah overstepped his authority by entering the temple to burn incense, which only the priests were authorized to burn. The LORD immediately struck him with leprosy, which he had until the day he died (2 Chronicles 26:16-23). In each one of these cases, the kings (State) crossed boundaries by taking over the responsibilities that belonged to the priests (Church).

In the New Testament, Jesus recognized the boundaries between church and state when he said, "Give to Caesar what is Caesar's, and to God what is God's" (Matthew 22:21). Caesar must be given his due, *but we may not give him what belongs to God*. If Caesar demands what belongs to God, we must resist. To obey Caesar in this would make us complicit in Caesar's transgression. Our obedience to Caesar would bring guilt before God.

Like the design of each sphere, the roles and responsibilities given to each sphere also proceed from the nature of God. Each community is to function as the Godhead functions. The primary responsibilities of the church are to promulgate the gospel, teach and disciple the flock, and provide for the needs of widows and orphans. Similarly, the family is responsible for procreation, education and discipling of children, and providing for family members. The responsibilities of the State differ from all the other social spheres. In every other sphere, there are responsibilities for education or training, and for making provision for others, but the State has a completely different role. The State takes on the role of God as Judge. Thus, the responsibilities of the State are to condone good and punish evil.

In order for the State to fulfill its purpose in God's plan, the State has to know what good and evil are. It is absolutely crucial that the Word of God informs the State on this matter. If the State takes its cues from anything other than the Word of God, the result will be death to its citizens. In other words, if the State puts itself in place of God, deciding on its own what is good, evil, right, or wrong, it is doomed to destruction. According to Romans 13, the State is the agent of God's wrath, and as such it bears the sword. As the sword-bearer, the State has an awesome power to protect and punish, but an evil State will use the sword indiscriminately against its own citizens. Because of this delegation of power, the State has the most potential to become an oppressor, and to set itself up in place of God. The State that does this becomes the anti-Christ in this world (1 John 4:3).

History bears witness to this fact. Nations founded on humanistic principles have ended up in tyrannous dictatorships where millions upon millions of innocent men, women, and children have been viciously slaughtered. Joseph Stalin was responsible for over forty million deaths. Mao Zedong was credited with over thirty-five million, and Adolf Hitler with over twenty million, just to mention a few. Over the course of time, nearly two hundred million unarmed, helpless citizens have been murdered in a myriad of ways by their own governments. When kings do not submit to God, the consequences are hell on earth.

What about the State that becomes a dictatorship by non-violent means? Is the transgression any less a sin? In the United States, the State has gradually taken control of what rightly belongs to the other spheres, not by violence, but through education. In doing so, the State has declared war on the family and the church, redefining marriage, approving of homosexual partnerships, promoting stem cell research, seducing us with welfare and health care, and finally, stealing children from parents with compulsory education laws. When the State can isolate children from their parents for thirty-five hours a week, it can educate them to believe anything it wants them to believe. Most people who have graduated from a State school in America believe that the State is the Grantor of Rights, that the State is responsible for welfare, health care, wage and price control, labor laws, and education.

When the State takes over control of the other spheres, the result is chaos. Boundary lines are crossed. Roles are reversed. God is out of the picture, and the State replaces God. Because of its enmity toward God, the State views God's design for church and family as repressive, intolerant, and even hateful. Jean-Jacques Rousseau once said, "Man was born free, but everywhere he is in chains." The *chains* he referred to were the chains of Christianity. This is nothing new. From the beginning of time, the State has been the one social sphere that has consistently rivaled God and sought to replace him. Read what the psalmist says:

Psalm 2

1 Why do the nations conspire
   and the peoples plot in vain?
2 The kings of the earth take their stand
   and the rulers gather together
   against the LORD
   and against his Anointed One.
3 "Let us break their chains," they say,
   "and throw off their fetters."
4 The One enthroned in heaven laughs;
   the LORD scoffs at them.
5 Then he rebukes them in his anger
   and terrifies them in his wrath, saying,
6 "I have installed my King
   on Zion, my holy hill."
7 I will proclaim the decree of the LORD :
   He said to me, "You are my Son;
   today I have become your Father.
8 Ask of me,
   and I will make the nations your inheritance,
   the ends of the earth your possession.
9 You will rule them with an iron scepter;
   you will dash them to pieces like pottery."
10 Therefore, you kings, be wise;
   be warned, you rulers of the earth.

Humanists are not the only ones who believe the State is our savior. Many Christians also have come to believe in the State as the rightful provider of all good things. We too have transferred our dependence from God to the State. Most Christians today have been educated by the State, and the State has been successful in changing our worldview.

Two Trees of Knowledge

Antonio Gramski advised Lenin and Stalin about how to conquer the West. He gave them a two-fold prescription: 1) Rid the public square and the public schools of the memory of God, and 2) Indoctrinate the masses with Marxist propaganda through the public education system. In other words, completely revise history.

For decades, groups like the ACLU have been successfully erasing the memory of God from the public square. Lawsuits abound contesting the rights of Christians to display religious artifacts. The Ten Commandments may not be displayed in federal buildings. City squares are decorated with sterile winter wrappings in place of nativities. School children have "winter programs" instead of traditional Christmas programs.

Textbooks have had every mention of true Christianity removed. Original documents have been altered to hide the fact that our country was founded by Christians who came here to glorify God. Instead, historical Christian people are made out to be ridiculous figures or downright evil. Our founding fathers are martyred in print, and past events are filtered through a politically correct lens that has strong anti-American bias.

God warns us in Scripture about the spiritual decline and social pathologies that will result if his boundaries are transgressed, but many Christians are simply unaware that God's design for the State does not include the education of his children. Sometimes Christians justify their use of the public schools by insisting that their school is an exception. They believe it is basically a Christian school because some of the teachers are Christians or because the children sing Christian songs. This reasoning is flawed. It does not take into consideration the reason God has set boundaries on the State: The State is God's agent of wrath and it bears the sword. *Even if the State were to sponsor Christian education and teach Christianity to our children, it would still be transgressing God's law.* Christianity must never be enforced by the one who bears the sword. The ethnic and ideological cleansing we witness in Muslim nations is a good example of why this biblical principle is so important.

God followed through on this principle when he refused to allow David to build the temple. David was a godly man. In fact, he is the only man the Bible calls "a man after God's own heart." David, as king, represented the State. He was a warrior, a sword-bearer. He loved God with all his heart and wanted to build a temple for God, but God said no. David could not build the temple because *the sword-bearer cannot build the church*. David was the agent of God's wrath. He had blood on his hands. David stayed within the boundaries of God's command, and the job of building the temple was given to his son Solomon.

Solomon was also a king, but God did an amazing thing in Solomon's day. God gave Solomon unprecedented peace on all sides during his reign and especially during the building of the temple. There was no adversary and no disaster. Second Chronicles 9:22-24 tells us, "King Solomon was greater in riches and wisdom than all the other kings of the earth. All the kings of the earth sought audience with Solomon to hear the wisdom God had put in his heart. Year after year, everyone who came brought a gift—articles of silver and gold, and robes, weapons and spices, and horses and mules." King Solomon was not called upon to bear the sword. His was a reign of truth and righteousness, a foreshadowing of the future reign of Christ on the new earth.

There is only one time in the history of Israel when the State took over the education of God's people. This was during the reign of Jeroboam (1 Kings 12:25-33; 2 Chronicles 11:13-17). As you recall, Jeroboam tore the northern ten tribes of Israel away from King Rehoboam. He decided that he could not allow the Israelites to return to Jerusalem for their feasts, because then they might return to Rehoboam. He rejected the priests of the LORD, and the priests and Levites from every district returned to Rehoboam along with all the

> *"The king who thinks he is God soon becomes the devil."*
>
> —*Dr. Del Tackett*
> *The Truth Project*

people who set their hearts on seeking the LORD. Meanwhile, Jeroboam set up two golden calves for the people to worship, and built altars on all the high places. He told the people that the golden calves delivered them from Egypt, and he held festivals in imitation of the ones God instituted in Judah. He appointed his own priests to offer sacrifices. Jeroboam effectively carried out the two-fold scheme of changing a nation's worldview: He eliminated the knowledge of God from the land, and he revised history. From that point on, the ten northern tribes lost their status as God's chosen people.

This is the predictable result when the State takes over education. There is a manifest conflict of interest as the State wrestles with God for supremacy. In order to change the worldview of a nation, the State has to train the minds of the next generation. Like King Jeroboam, the State appoints its own teachers, rejecting the parents who are appointed by God. Like King Jeroboam, the State revises history. The State takes what it has no right to take.

Jesus said, "Give to Caesar what is Caesar's and to God what is God's." The Pharisees had tried to trap him, asking if it was right to pay taxes to Caesar, who was given the obeisance of a god. If Jesus said "yes," he would be acknowledging Caesar's right to divine status. If he said "no," they could have him arrested as a traitor. Instead of answering their question, he asked them for the coin used to pay the tax. On the coin was the image and inscription of Caesar. It was on this basis that he said "give to Caesar what is Caesar's and to God what is God's."

Parents, look at your children. The image of God is imprinted on them. They are his children. They do not belong to us and they do not belong to the State. When we allow the State access to what is rightfully God's, we cross a boundary line that puts our children in grave danger. When we cross that line, we put God to the test.

When Satan tempted Jesus, he took him to the highest point of the temple and encouraged him to jump down. Satan said, "It is written, 'He will command his angels concerning you, and they will lift you up in their hands so that you will not strike your foot against a stone.'"[35] Jesus answered him, "It is also written: 'Do not put the LORD your God to the test'" (Deuteronomy 6:16). Yet how often we hear parents say, "We know the public schools are bad, but we just pray that God will protect our children." We would not do

> *When we deliberately step outside the boundary lines that God has drawn for us, God has no obligation to answer our prayers.*

this with their physical safety. No parent in his right mind would set his toddler on a highway and then have the audacity to pray for God's protection. It is sheer lunacy to think that God would honor such a prayer. Yet we think nothing of putting them in spiritual danger every day, and the consequences are far worse. When we deliberately step outside the boundary lines that God has drawn for us, God has no obligation to answer our prayers. Instead, God gives us these warnings:

> You yourselves know how we lived in Egypt and how we passed through the countries on the way here. You saw among them their detestable images and idols of wood and stone, of silver and gold. Make sure there is no man or woman, clan or tribe among you today whose heart turns away from the LORD our God to go and worship the gods of those nations; make sure there is no root among you that produces such bitter poison.
>
> When such a person hears the words of this oath, he invokes a blessing on himself and therefore thinks, "I will be safe, even though I persist in going my own way." This will bring disaster on the watered land as well as the dry. The LORD will never be willing to forgive him; his wrath and zeal will burn against that man. All the curses written in this book will fall upon him, and the LORD will blot out his name from under heaven. The LORD will single him out from all the tribes of Israel for disaster, according to all the curses of the covenant written in this Book of the Law.
>
> —Deuteronomy 29:16-21

Two Trees of Knowledge

We will not be safe if we persist in going our own way. The consequences for our stubbornness can bring God's curse for all eternity. Even so, many parents are willing to play the odds.

Today in America, Christians play fast and loose with the Word of God. We would like to believe that we can transform the culture by keeping Christianity in the State schools. We persuade a music teacher to do Christian Christmas carols, and then rejoice in our "moral victory." What have we accomplished? We have not taught the children that Christianity is the only way; we have merely taught them that Christianity should not be excluded from the pluralistic secularism of our pagan culture. We are doing what the Samaritans did—they continued to worship their own gods, but added the LORD to the mix. We are not Christianizing the culture, we are adulterating Christianity. Plastering a Christian veneer on a pagan institution and calling it a Christian victory is the moral equivalent of nailing crossbars to an Asherah pole and calling it a cross. Radical Christianity demands that we cut down the Asherah pole and put up the cross in its place. *That* is transforming the culture. That is the path God is calling us to walk.

In ancient times, it was not enough for the people to merely abandon the Asherah poles and the high places. The Asherah poles had to be cut down and the high places had to be destroyed, because they were a continual snare to the people (2 Chronicles 6:2-6). Jesus said "If your eye causes you to sin, gouge it out and throw it away" (Matthew 18:9). Notice, he didn't say, "close your eye," but "gouge it out." This is radical theology, and what it means for us is this: Ultimately, it is not enough that we abandon the State schools. We must work toward abolishing them, because as long as they are in existence, they will be a snare to Christians who are tempted to take the easy way out—using others' resources to educate their children and succumbing to the seduction of the extracurricular packaging. We must work to privatize education for everyone—according to God's perfect design. We must take back our God-given role. We must stop looking at this as a punishment and see it for what it is, a privilege.

It is a privilege for people to train their own children in their own way. It is a privilege for parents *of any persuasion* to pass on the language, traditions, and religious beliefs that have been handed down from generation to generation. It is an honor and a privilege to be chosen of God to bring your own child into the faith. It is our responsibility as Christians to make sure that all parents have the right to train their own children in the way they see fit. The State has taken this right away. It has declared war on the family. It is time to fight back.

Here is one final warning God gives which should give every parent pause: "My people are destroyed from lack of knowledge. Because you have rejected knowledge, I also reject you as my priests; because you have ignored the law of your God, I also will ignore your children" (Hosea 4:6). If we continue to ignore the *whole* law of God, if we continue to play fast and loose with God's decrees, if we continue to overstep the boundaries and ignore the design that God has given for each of the social spheres, our children will pay the price…for all eternity.

Soli Deo Gloria

FURTHER UP
AND
FURTHER IN

WEEK FIVE—DAY ONE

Warnings

KNOWLEDGE:

1 Samuel 8

When Samuel grew old, he appointed his sons as judges for Israel. The name of his firstborn was Joel and the name of his second was Abijah, and they served at Beersheba. But his sons did not walk in his ways. They turned aside after dishonest gain and accepted bribes and perverted justice. So all the elders of Israel gathered together and came to Samuel at Ramah. They said to him, "You are old, and your sons do not walk in your ways; now appoint a king to lead us, such as all the other nations have." But when they said, "Give us a king to lead us," this displeased Samuel; so he prayed to the LORD.

And the LORD told him: "Listen to all that the people are saying to you; it is not you they have rejected, but they have rejected me as their king. As they have done from the day I brought them up out of Egypt until this day, forsaking me and serving other gods, so they are doing to you. Now listen to them; but warn them solemnly and let them know what the king who will reign over them will do." Samuel told all the words of the LORD to the people who were asking him for a king.

He said, "This is what the king who will reign over you will do: He will take your sons and make them serve with his chariots and horses, and they will run in front of his chariots. Some he will assign to be commanders of thousands and commanders of fifties, and others to plow his ground and reap his harvest, and still others to make weapons of war and equipment for his chariots. He will take your daughters to be perfumers and cooks and bakers. He will take the best of your fields and vineyards and olive groves and give them to his attendants. He will take a tenth of your grain and of your vintage and give it to his officials and attendants. Your menservants and maidservants and the best of your cattle and donkeys he will take for his own use. He will take a tenth of your flocks, and you yourselves will become his slaves.

When that day comes, you will cry out for relief from the king you have chosen, and the LORD will not answer you in that day." But the people refused to listen to Samuel. "No!" they said. "We want a king over us. Then we will be like all the other nations, with a king to lead us and to go out before us and fight our battles." When Samuel heard all that the people said, he repeated it before the LORD. The LORD answered, "Listen to them and give them a king." Then Samuel said to the men of Israel, "Everyone go back to his town."

UNDERSTANDING:

1. Why did the people ask for a king?
2. Whom were they replacing?
3. What are the first two things the king will demand from the people?
4. How does the king steal wealth and redistribute it? Does he give it to the poor?

WISDOM:

How does our government compare with God's description of the State?

NOTES

WEEK FIVE—DAY TWO

Boundaries

KNOWLEDGE:

Deuteronomy 17:14-15, 18-20

When you enter the land the LORD your God is giving you and have taken possession of it and settled in it, and you say, "Let us set a king over us like all the nations around us," be sure to appoint over you the king the LORD your God chooses... When he takes the throne of his kingdom, he is to write for himself on a scroll a copy of this law, taken from that of the priests, who are Levites. It is to be with him, and he is to read it all the days of his life so that he may learn to revere the LORD his God and follow carefully all the words of this law and these decrees and not consider himself better than his brothers and turn from the law to the right or to the left. Then he and his descendants will reign a long time over his kingdom in Israel.

2 Chronicles 19:4-10

Jehoshaphat lived in Jerusalem, and he went out again among the people from Beersheba to the hill country of Ephraim and turned them back to the LORD, the God of their fathers. He appointed judges in the land, in each of the fortified cities of Judah. He told them, "Consider carefully what you do, because you are not judging for man but for the LORD, who is with you whenever you give a verdict. Now let the fear of the LORD be upon you. Judge carefully, for with the LORD our God there is no injustice or partiality or bribery." In Jerusalem also, Jehoshaphat appointed some of the Levites, priests and heads of Israelite families to administer the law of the LORD and to settle disputes. And they lived in Jerusalem. He gave them these orders: "You must serve faithfully and wholeheartedly in the fear of the LORD. In every case that comes before you from your fellow countrymen who live in the cities—whether bloodshed or other concerns of the law, commands, decrees or ordinances—you are to warn them not to sin against the LORD; otherwise his wrath will come on you and your brothers. Do this, and you will not sin.

Matthew 22:21

Give to Caesar what is Caesar's and to God what is God's.

Romans 13:3-6

For rulers hold no terror for those who do right, but for those who do wrong. Do you want to be free from fear of the one in authority? Then do what is right and he will commend you. For he is God's servant to do you good. But if you do wrong, be afraid, for he does not bear the sword for nothing. He is God's servant, an agent of wrath to bring punishment on the wrongdoer. Therefore, it is necessary to submit to the authorities, not only because of possible punishment but also because of conscience. This is also why you pay taxes, for the authorities are God's servants, who give their full time to governing.

1 Peter 2:13-14

Submit yourselves for the Lord's sake to every authority instituted among men: whether to the king, as the supreme authority, or to governors, who are sent by him to punish those who do wrong and to commend those who do right.

UNDERSTANDING:

1. What are the duties of the governing authorities? To what must the State give its full time according to Romans 13?
2. Are there any scriptural grounds for the State taking over the education of children?
3. Is the State responsible to follow and enforce the laws that God has set up or is the State supposed to make laws of its own?

WISDOM:

1. Each social sphere has boundaries put in place by God. When the boundaries are crossed, it constitutes sin. When Jesus said that what belongs to God should never be given to Caesar, he was reinforcing the principle of sphere sovereignty, of the boundaries between church and state. Keeping this in mind, is it a sin for Christians to send their children to State schools?
2. What are some of the pathologies that result when boundaries are crossed?

NOTES

_____

_____

_____

_____

_____

_____

_____

_____

_____

_____

_____

_____

_____

_____

Week Five—Day Three

God's Sovereignty over Nations

KNOWLEDGE:

Exodus 9:13-16

Then the LORD said to Moses, "Get up early in the morning, confront Pharaoh and say to him, 'This is what the LORD, the God of the Hebrews, says: Let my people go, so that they may worship me, or this time I will send the full force of my plagues against you and against your officials and your people, so you may know that there is no one like me in all the earth. For by now I could have stretched out my hand and struck you and your people with a plague that would have wiped you off the earth. But I have raised you up for this very purpose, that I might show you my power and that my name might be proclaimed in all the earth.'"

Isaiah 10:5-7,12-13

Woe to the Assyrian, the rod of my anger, in whose hand is the club of my wrath! I send him against a godless nation, I dispatch him against a people who anger me, to seize loot and snatch plunder, and to trample them down like mud in the streets. But this is not what he intends, this is not what he has in mind; his purpose is to destroy, to put an end to many nations.

When the LORD has finished all his work against Mount Zion and Jerusalem, he will say, "I will punish the king of Assyria for the willful pride of his heart and the haughty look in his eyes. For he says: 'By the strength of my hand I have done this, and by my wisdom, because I have understanding. I removed the boundaries of nations, I plundered their treasures; like a mighty one I subdued their kings.'"

Acts 17:24-26

The God who made the world and everything in it is the LORD of heaven and earth and does not live in temples built by hands. And he is not served by human hands, as if he needed anything, because he himself gives all men life and breath and everything else. From one man he made every nation of men, that they should inhabit the whole earth; and he determined the times set for them and the exact places where they should live.

UNDERSTANDING:

1. Is God the authority over only those kings who are Christian or who rule over Christian nations?
2. Do kings and rulers necessarily realize that God is directing their steps?
3. If an ungodly king does not understand or recognize God's authority, will he be punished anyway?

WISDOM:

Discuss ways in which our government has denied the design of God for the sphere of the State.

NOTES

WEEK FIVE—DAY FOUR

To Obey or Not to Obey

KNOWLEDGE:

Jeremiah 25:27-31

Then tell them, "This is what the LORD Almighty, the God of Israel, says: Drink, get drunk and vomit, and fall to rise no more because of the sword I will send among you." But if they refuse to take the cup from your hand and drink, tell them, "This is what the LORD Almighty says: You must drink it! See, I am beginning to bring disaster on the city that bears my Name, and will you indeed go unpunished? You will not go unpunished, for I am calling down a sword upon all who live on the earth, declares the LORD Almighty." Now prophesy all these words against them and say to them: "The LORD will roar from on high; he will thunder from his holy dwelling and roar mightily against his land. He will shout like those who tread the grapes, shout against all who live on the earth. The tumult will resound to the ends of the earth, for the LORD will bring charges against the nations; he will bring judgment on all mankind and put the wicked to the sword," declares the LORD.

John 6:8

For I have come down from heaven not to do my will but to do the will of him who sent me.

Matthew 7:21

Not everyone who says to me, "Lord, Lord," will enter the kingdom of heaven, but only he who does the will of my Father who is in heaven.

Acts 5:29

Peter and the other apostles replied: "We must obey God rather than men!"

UNDERSTANDING:

1. Whose will are we to carry out in everything we do?
2. What are the consequences for disobedience to God's will?

WISDOM:

1. According to the above verses, blind obedience to the will of the State can lead to eternal consequences. God will punish the nation that follows depraved leaders. In what areas has the State in America set itself up as a rival to God?
2. How should Christians address these issues?

NOTES

WEEK FIVE—DAY FIVE

Offense or Defense?

KNOWLEDGE:

Deuteronomy 7:1-2

When the LORD your God brings you into the land you are entering to possess and drives out before you many nations—the Hittites, Girgashites, Amorites, Canaanites, Perizzites, Hivites and Jebusites, seven nations larger and stronger than you—and when the LORD your God has delivered them over to you and you have defeated them, then you must destroy them totally. Make no treaty with them, and show them no mercy.

2 Chronicles 6:2-6

Asa did what was good and right in the eyes of the LORD his God. He removed the foreign altars and the high places, smashed the sacred stones and cut down the Asherah poles. He commanded Judah to seek the LORD, the God of their fathers, and to obey his laws and commands. He removed the high places and incense altars in every town in Judah, and the kingdom was at peace under him. He built up the fortified cities of Judah, since the land was at peace. No one was at war with him during those years, for the LORD gave him rest.

Matthew 16:18 (ESV)

And I tell you, you are Peter, and on this rock I will build my church, and the gates of hell shall not prevail against it.

Ephesians 6:11-12

Put on the full armor of God so that you can take your stand against the devil's schemes. For our struggle is not against flesh and blood, but against the rulers, against the authorities, against the powers of this dark world and against the spiritual forces of evil in the heavenly realms.

UNDERSTANDING:

1. When the Israelites entered Canaan, did they wait for their neighbors to attack them or did they attack first?
2. What actions did King Asa take against spiritual enemies in the land? What did he do during the time of peace God gave him?
3. When Jesus said, "the gates of hell shall not prevail against it" (the church), was he assuming the church was on the offense or the defense?

WISDOM:

1. Should Christians wait until they are assaulted by evil before taking up arms?
2. According to the principles of 2 Chronicles 6:2-6, is it enough for Christians to merely leave the public schools, or should we work to abolish them?
3. In what ways should Christians be more proactive on issues like abortion, the homosexual agenda, and the takeover of the education of our children by the State?
4. Since we are not going to literally kill our enemies, what would a pre-emptive strike look like? (Reference Ephesians Chapter 6)

NOTES

Chapter 6

Deadly Alliances

You adulterous people, don't you know that friendship with the world is hatred toward God? Anyone who chooses to be a friend of the world becomes an enemy of God.

—James 4:4

IN PAUL'S TIME, the city of Corinth was a strategic commercial center that sought to provide international pleasures. The Christians in Corinth were polarized over the issue of association with sinners, some believing that such associations were permissible and necessary, others believing that a certain measure of isolation was essential to the preservation of holiness. These opposing views grew out of control and threatened the future of the church in Corinth. Paul addressed this issue in 2 Corinthians 6:14-18:

> Do not be yoked together with unbelievers. For what do righteousness and wickedness have in common? Or what fellowship can light have with darkness? What harmony is there between Christ and Belial? What does a believer have in common with an unbeliever? What agreement is there between the temple of God and idols? For we are

the temple of the living God. As God has said: "I will live with them and walk among them, and I will be their God, and they will be my people.

"Therefore come out from them
 and be separate, says the Lord.
 Touch no unclean thing,
 and I will receive you."
"I will be a Father to you,
 and you will be my sons and daughters, says the Lord Almighty."

When Paul wrote his letter to the Corinthians, warning them not to be unequally yoked with unbelievers, this was not a new concept. Paul was drawing on an ancient principle dating back to the time of Abraham, when God chose a people to be his treasured possession. He called them to be holy, separate from the world. There were two reasons for this call to separation. One was the threat of intermarriage with foreigners. This was a danger on two counts: 1) Intermarriage would threaten the pure genealogical line from which the Messiah would be born, and 2) Foreign wives would seduce the Israelites into worshipping other gods.

The second reason was that proximity to other nations would cause the Israelites to learn their ways, to desire what they had, and to mimic their lifestyles. They might also make treaties and alliances with them during war instead of depending solely on God. The consequences for these alliances, no matter how far removed from their personal lives, would prove deadly. One theme consistently reappears throughout Scripture: Any kind of alliance with the world, no matter how insignificant it may seem, is a threat to our relationship with God. God is not saying that we should have no association with unbelievers. What he is warning us against are situations where a believer gives significant control over his actions to an unbeliever. This would include covenants like marriage, business partnerships, contracts, alliances, treaties, or any affiliation in which unbelievers can impose their will on believers. Moses warned the Israelites:

> Be careful, or you will be enticed to turn away and worship other gods and bow down to them. Then the LORD's anger will burn against you, and he will shut the heavens so that it will not rain and the ground will yield no produce, and you will soon perish from the good land the LORD is giving you.
>
> —Deuteronomy 11:16-17

> The LORD your God will cut off before you the nations you are about to invade and dispossess. But when you have driven them out and settled in their land, and after they have been destroyed before you, be careful not to be ensnared by inquiring about their gods, saying, "How do these nations serve their gods? We will do the same." You must not worship the LORD your God in their way, because in worshipping their gods, they do all kinds of detestable things the LORD hates. They even burn their sons and daughters in the fire as sacrifices to their gods.
>
> —Deuteronomy 12:29-31

> You are the children of the LORD your God. Do not cut yourselves or shave the front of your heads for the dead, for you are a people holy to the LORD your God. Out of all the peoples on the face of the earth, the LORD has chosen you to be his treasured possession.
>
> —Deuteronomy 14:1-2

> When you enter the land the LORD your God is giving you, do not learn to imitate the detestable ways of the nations there. Let no one be found among you who sacrifices his son or daughter in the fire, who practices divination or sorcery, interprets omens, engages in witchcraft, or casts spells, or who is a medium or spiritist or who consults the dead. Anyone who does these things is detestable to the LORD, and because of these detestable practices the LORD your God

will drive out those nations before you. You must be blameless before the LORD your God.

—Deuteronomy 18:9-14

Consecrate yourselves and be holy, because I am the LORD your God. Keep my decrees and follow them. I am the LORD, who makes you holy.

—Leviticus 20:7

At a later time King Solomon gave the following advice:

Do not set foot on the path of the wicked
or walk in the way of evil men

Avoid it, do not travel on it;
turn from it and go on your way.

Let your eyes look straight ahead,
fix your gaze directly before you.

Make level paths for your feet
and take only ways that are firm.

Do not swerve to the right or the left;
keep your foot from evil.

—Proverbs 4:14-15, 25-27

In spite of all these warnings, even the most God-fearing people take what they believe to be just a tiny little detour from the right path. They believe the consequences for a "minor indiscretion" will be minimal. King Jehoshaphat of Judah is a perfect example.[36]

King Jehoshaphat was one of only a few God-fearing kings in Judah. Scripture records that Jehoshaphat "did what was right in the eyes of the LORD." He rid the land of male shrine prostitutes, he tore down the Asherah poles, he refused to consult the Baals, and he sought to follow God's commands as David had done. Jehoshaphat made sure that the law of God was taught in every part of Judah. As a result, God established Jehoshaphat's kingdom, bringing him great wealth, honor, and peace. Jehoshaphat became very powerful and neighboring kings brought him gifts.

During Jehoshaphat's reign in Judah, Ahab was the king of Israel, which had become a pagan nation, rejecting God and worshipping idols. Ahab was married to Jezebel, renowned for her extreme wickedness. Jehoshaphat went down to visit Ahab—his first mistake. While he was there, he arranged a marriage for his son with Ahab's daughter, his second mistake. Ahab then asked him to join with him in battle against Ramoth Gilead. Jehoshaphat replied, "I am as you are, my people as your people, my horses as your horses." Although Jehoshaphat insisted that they consult a prophet of the LORD, he was clearly in the wrong for making such an alliance. Jehu, the seer, came to confront him with these words: "Should you help the wicked and love those who hate the LORD? Because of this, the wrath of the LORD is on you." As a discipline and a warning, the LORD sent the Moabites to war against Jehoshaphat. Jehoshaphat and the people repented, and God relented, fighting the battle for them as they stood by and watched.

Jehoshaphat, however, had not learned his lesson. After Ahab's death, he made an alliance with Ahab's son, Ahaziah, to build a fleet of ships for trade. Once again, a prophet of the LORD came to Jehoshaphat saying, "Because you have made an alliance with Ahaziah, the LORD will destroy what you have made." Every ship in the fleet was wrecked. Jehoshaphat's fourth alliance was with Joram, another son of Ahab who reigned over Israel after Ahaziah died. This time Israel and Judah joined forces to war against Moab. Each time Jehoshaphat made an alliance with Israel, God brought judgment on him.

Jehoshaphat made alliances that involved both personal relationships and international affairs of state. Many of the consequences for these alliances came much later, but they were deadly, nearly annihilating the house of David through which the promised Messiah would come.

Jehoram, Jehoshaphat's son, ruled Judah after the death of his father. He married Athaliah, a daughter of Ahab and Jezebel, as Jehoshaphat had arranged. Scripture tells us he "walked in the ways of the kings of Israel as the house of Ahab had done." He murdered all the princes of Judah as well as some of the princes of Israel. God inflicted him with a disease of the bowels and he died a slow painful death—"his bowels came out and he died in great pain." Scripture then adds this sorry note: "He passed away to no one's regret." The people did not build a fire in his honor and he was not buried with the kings.

After Jehoram's death, his son Ahaziah became king. Unsurprisingly, he went to Israel to visit Israel's king, Joram, who had been wounded in battle. Scripture says, "Through Ahaziah's visit to Joram, God brought about Ahaziah's downfall." God sent Jehu to destroy the whole family of Ahab, and while he was at it, he also killed Ahaziah and his sons.

When Ahaziah was killed, his mother Athaliah (Jezebel's daughter) proceeded to destroy the whole royal family of the house of Judah, so she could usurp the throne. This evil woman methodically set about murdering her own grandchildren! Had she succeeded, the line of David would have been extinguished, and the line of Christ destroyed. However, a one-year old baby was rescued by the wife of a priest. He was hidden away until he could become king.

Jehoshaphat was known as one of the most righteous kings ever to rule Israel. Yet his one outstanding sin was making alliances with the pagan kings of Israel. His son and daughter-in-law rivaled Ahab and Jezebel in wickedness. Most of his descendents were lost for all eternity because of his indiscretions. One weakness destroyed his family. Martin Luther once said,

> If I profess with the loudest voice and clearest exposition every portion of the truth of God except precisely that little point which the world and the devil are at that moment attacking, I am not confessing Christ, however boldly I may be professing Christ. Where the battle rages there the loyalty of the soldier is proved and to be steady on

all the battlefields besides is mere flight and disgrace if he flinches at that one point.[37]

Jehoshaphat failed at just one point, but it cost his family dearly. God's intervention was the only thing that prevented the total annihilation of his descendents.

About three hundred years later, just before Judah was taken into captivity, God sent Jeremiah to give the people one last chance. Jeremiah pleads, "Do not learn the ways of the nations…" It is amazing that even after all their adulteries, God is still pleading with his people and giving them another chance to avoid catastrophe. In every warning we see the phrase, "Do not learn…" What goes into our minds is of supreme importance to God. We are to love him with all our minds. Every scriptural prohibition against intermingling with the world is connected with learning the ways of the world.

The prohibition against unequal yoking includes parents partnering with the State to educate their children. When parents do this, they give the State a very significant amount of control over decisions concerning their children. Consider this November 2, 2005 statement by the Ninth Circuit Court of Appeals:

> Once parents make the choice as to which school their children will attend…their fundamental right to control the education of their children is, at the least, substantially diminished. The Constitution does not vest parents with the authority to interfere with a public school's decision as to how it will provide information to its students or what information it will provide, in its classroom or otherwise… Perhaps the Sixth Court said it best when it explained,

> While parents may have a fundamental right to decide whether to send their child to a public school, they do not have a fundamental right generally to direct how a public school teaches their child. Whether it is the school curriculum, the hours of the school day, school discipline,

the timing and content of examinations, the individuals hired to teach at the school, the extracurricular activities offered at the school or, as here, a dress code, these issues of public education are generally 'committed to the control of state and local authorities.'"[38]

When we allow the State to educate our children, the State usurps our authority over them: The State determines the age at which children will begin their education, it determines how many days a year the children will sit in the classroom, it determines how many years they must attend, it determines the career path that will be open for each student, it determines when a child is in need of counseling, it determines which vaccinations will be required, and most importantly, it determines the content of the curriculum. *These things are all determined without the consent of a child's parents, often in spite of the parents' desires.* School social workers are allowed to counsel children without informing the parents. Schools can report parents to family services if parents refuse to medicate a student who doesn't conform to their program. In one such incident, a principal in a rural Kansas school district told a concerned mother, "When you enroll your child in our school, you play by our rules, and our rules do not allow for parental input." When the State exercises this kind of control, then God's injunction, "do not be unequally yoked with unbelievers" applies.

When parents partner with the State to train the minds of their children, they are yoked together with unbelievers for the single most important job they have as parents. Do not be deceived into thinking you are partnering with the nice teacher. Behind every teacher is a State-sanctioned curriculum that certified teachers are bound by law to teach. Behind the State-sanctioned curriculum stands the enemy of our souls. He prowls around like a roaring lion seeking to devour his prey. Children are easy prey. God calls us to partner *with him* in the training of our little ones. It is the thing we agree to do, *vow* to do when we have them baptized or dedicated. He does not take it lightly when we adulterate that covenant to partner instead with the State in the education of his children.

When God commands us to make no alliances with the world, he means it—even when it seems safe. Jehoshaphat made no alliances with other kings as far as we know. Could it be that he was seduced into thinking that Israel was "safe" just because they were once God's people? Did he think of them as brothers? Did he think God would understand? God warned him time after time, but he never learned his lesson. Is God warning us today?

The New Testament gives the same warnings to us that God gave Israel in the Old Testament. Peter restates our holy calling, "But you are a chosen people, a royal priesthood, a holy nation, a people belonging to God, that you may declare the praises of him *who called you out of darkness into his wonderful light.*"(1 Peter 2:9) James writes, "You adulterous people, don't you know that friendship with the world is hatred toward God? *Anyone who chooses to be a friend of the world becomes an enemy of God*" (James 4:4). John adds, "Do not love the world or anything in the world. *If anyone loves the world, the love of the Father is not in him*" (1 John 2:15). Jesus himself voices the great divorce between believers and the world: "If the world hates you, keep in mind that it hated me first. If you belonged to the world, it would love you as its own. *As it is, you do not belong to the world.* That is why the world hates you" (John 15:18-19). The State schools are the world's training grounds. Our children do not belong there.

Jesus specifically warns us about State-sanctioned teaching. "Be careful," Jesus warned them, "Watch out for the yeast of the Pharisees *and that of Herod*" (Mark 8:15). This is pivotal, because Jesus is telling us that sitting under the tutelage of the State is just as dangerous as sitting under the tutelage of religious heretics. The implication of Jesus' warning is clear: we are not to make educational alliances with either.

Many parents say that they have no choice but to send their children to State schools. God will not accept that as an excuse. It may cost dearly in time and inconvenience and money, but it is a lie to say we have no choice. If we are totally honest, most parents who utilize the State schools do it because it is convenient, it is mostly paid for by others, and parents get "free" forty-hour-a-week child care so they can pursue their own goals. As an additional bonus, they get awesome sports programs and extra-curricular activities. Christians beware: When you enroll your children in the State schools, you are making a pact with the devil. All these benefits have a price: the minds of your children. Is it worth the risk of losing them forever?

God warns us about alliances with unbelievers in Scripture because he knows how susceptible we are to deception. He knows that if we believe a lie, it will lead us into sin. All lies lead to sin. Our beliefs determine our actions. Jesus said, "But if anyone causes one of these little ones who believe in me to sin, it would be better for him to have a large millstone hung around his neck and to be drowned in the depths of the sea" (Matthew 8:6). Jesus is specifically referring to covenant children here, children who believe in him. Children who are taught lies will be led into sin. That is why it is extremely important for parents who send their children to school, to delegate the teaching to those who will promote the Christian worldview to their children. Remember fathers, God holds you personally responsible for whatever your children learn. If you delegate that responsibility, it had better be to someone who would teach them what you would teach them at home. If you delegate that responsibility to the State, and your child is one of the seventy-five to ninety percent who reject the faith, the proverbial millstone is for your neck.

There are parents who believe they can beat the odds. It is human nature to believe that our children will listen to us and become like us. But our reasoning is flawed and Jesus debunks that kind of thinking when he says, "A student is not above his teacher, but everyone who is fully trained will be *like his teacher*." The statistics are proving Jesus true. Our children are turning out like their teachers.

God is calling us to serve him and only him. We cannot worship God on Sundays and then serve the State the rest of the week, and serving the State is exactly what we do every time we submit to its rules concerning the welfare of our children. Serving the State is what we do when we allow it to determine the content of our children's curriculum, a curriculum that is turning them away from the faith in record numbers. The ungodly alliances we make are deadly. God has warned us. The prophets have spoken. They are speaking today. Do we have ears to hear?

Soli Deo Gloria

FURTHER UP
AND
FURTHER IN

WEEK SIX—DAY ONE

Unequally Yoked

KNOWLEDGE:

Deuteronomy 14:1-2

You are the children of the LORD your God. Do not cut yourselves or shave the front of your heads for the dead, for you are a people holy to the LORD your God. Out of all the peoples on the face of the earth, the LORD has chosen you to be his treasured possession.

2 Corinthians 6:14-18

Do not be yoked together with unbelievers. For what do righteousness and wickedness have in common? Or what fellowship can light have with darkness? What harmony is there between Christ and Belial? What does a believer have in common with an unbeliever? What agreement is there between the temple of God and idols? For we are the temple of the living God. As God has said: "I will live with them and walk among them, and I will be their God, and they will be my people."

"Therefore come out from them
and be separate, says the Lord.
Touch no unclean thing,
and I will receive you."
"I will be a Father to you,
and you will be my sons and daughters, says the Lord Almighty."

Leviticus 20:7

"Consecrate yourselves and be holy, because I am the LORD your God. Keep my decrees and follow them. I am the LORD, who makes you holy."

1 Peter 2:9

But you are a chosen people, a royal priesthood, a holy nation, a people belonging to God, that you may declare the praises of him who called you out of darkness into his wonderful light.

Psalm 1:1

Blessed is the man who does not walk in the counsel of the wicked, or stand in the way of sinners or sit in the seat of mockers.

UNDERSTANDING:

1. Why does God forbid us to be in associations or partnerships with unbelievers where we willingly give them significant control over our actions and decisions?
2. How would this principle apply to student-teacher relationships?
3. Does this mean we should never have anything to do with unbelievers?

WISDOM:

God gave the responsibility of raising and educating children to parents because he wanted "godly offspring." When parents delegate areas of that responsibility to someone else, they are asking someone to partner with them in doing their job. According to the verses above, do you think it is a sin to delegate that responsibility to unbelievers?

NOTES

WEEK SIX—DAY TWO

Lot

KNOWLEDGE:

Genesis 13:11-13

So Lot chose for himself the whole plain of the Jordan and set out toward the east. The two men parted company: Abram lived in the land of Canaan, while Lot lived among the cities of the plain and pitched his tents near Sodom. Now the men of Sodom were wicked and were sinning greatly against the LORD.

Genesis 14:11-12

The four kings seized all the goods of Sodom and Gomorrah and all their food; then they went away. They also carried off Abram's nephew Lot and his possessions, since he was living in Sodom.

Genesis 19:1; 12-26

The two angels arrived at Sodom in the evening, and Lot was sitting in the gateway of the city. When he saw them, he got up to meet them and bowed down with his face to the ground...

The two men said to Lot, "Do you have anyone else here—sons-in-law, sons or daughters, or anyone else in the city who belongs to you? Get them out of here, because we are going to destroy this place. The outcry to the LORD against its people is so great that he has sent us to destroy it."

So Lot went out and spoke to his sons-in-law, who were pledged to marry his daughters. He said, "Hurry and get out of this place, because the LORD is about to destroy the city!" But his sons-in-law thought he was joking.

With the coming of dawn, the angels urged Lot, saying, "Hurry! Take your wife and your two daughters who are here, or you will be swept away when the city is punished."

When he hesitated, the men grasped his hand and the hands of his wife and of his two daughters and led them safely out of the city, for the LORD was merciful to them. As soon as they had brought them out, one of them said, "Flee for your lives! Don't look back, and don't stop anywhere in the plain! Flee to the mountains or you will be swept away!"

But Lot said to them, "No, my lords, please! Your servant has found favor in your eyes, and you have shown great kindness to me in sparing my life. But I can't flee to the mountains; this disaster will overtake me, and I'll die. Look, here is a town near enough to run to, and it is small. Let me flee to it—it is very small, isn't it? Then my life will be spared."

He said to him, "Very well, I will grant this request too; I will not overthrow the town you speak of. But flee there quickly, because I cannot do anything until you reach it." (That is why the town was called Zoar.)

By the time Lot reached Zoar, the sun had risen over the land. Then the LORD rained down burning sulfur on Sodom and Gomorrah—from the LORD out of the heavens. Thus he overthrew those cities and the entire plain, including all those living in the cities—and also the vegetation in the land. But Lot's wife looked back, and she became a pillar of salt.

UNDERSTANDING:

1. Where did Lot start out in relation to Sodom?
2. What happened to him when he moved into the city?
3. Did he learn his lesson?
4. Why do you think he stayed in the city according to Genesis 19:1?
5. Did Lot's presence in the city influence anyone to honor God?
6. When God destroyed the city, did Lot lose any family members?

WISDOM:

1. Do you think Lot and his wife believed they could be a godly influence in the city?
2. Why was that impossible?
3. What principles can we apply to our lives from the story of Lot?

NOTES

WEEK SIX—DAY THREE

Dinah

KNOWLEDGE:

Genesis 34

Now Dinah, the daughter Leah had borne to Jacob, went out to visit the women of the land. When Shechem son of Hamor the Hivite, the ruler of that area, saw her, he took her and violated her. His heart was drawn to Dinah daughter of Jacob, and he loved the girl and spoke tenderly to her. And Shechem said to his father Hamor, "Get me this girl as my wife."

When Jacob heard that his daughter Dinah had been defiled, his sons were in the fields with his livestock; so he kept quiet about it until they came home.

Then Shechem's father Hamor went out to talk with Jacob. Now Jacob's sons had come in from the fields as soon as they heard what had happened. They were filled with grief and fury, because Shechem had done a disgraceful thing in Israel by lying with Jacob's daughter—a thing that should not be done.

But Hamor said to them, "My son Shechem has his heart set on your daughter. Please give her to him as his wife. Intermarry with us; give us your daughters and take our daughters for yourselves. You can settle among us; the land is open to you. Live in it, trade in it, and acquire property in it."

Then Shechem said to Dinah's father and brothers, "Let me find favor in your eyes, and I will give you whatever you ask. Make the price for the bride and the gift I am to bring as great as you like, and I'll pay whatever you ask me. Only give me the girl as my wife."

Because their sister Dinah had been defiled, Jacob's sons replied deceitfully as they spoke to Shechem and his father Hamor. They said to them, "We can't do such a thing; we can't give our sister to a man who is not circumcised. That would be a disgrace to us. We will give our consent to you on one condition only: that you become like us by circumcising all your males. Then we will give you our daughters and take your daughters for ourselves. We'll settle among you and become one people with you. But if you will not agree to be circumcised, we'll take our sister and go."

Their proposal seemed good to Hamor and his son Shechem. The young man, who was the most honored of all his father's household, lost no time in doing what they said, because he was delighted with Jacob's daughter. So Hamor and his son Shechem went to the gate of their city to speak to their fellow townsmen. "These men are friendly toward us," they said. "Let them live in our land and trade in it; the land has plenty of room for them. We can marry their daughters and they can marry ours. But the men will consent to live with us as one people only on the condition that our males be circumcised, as they themselves are. Won't their livestock, their property and all their other animals become ours? So let us give our consent to them, and they will settle among us."

All the men who went out of the city gate agreed with Hamor and his son Shechem, and every male in the city was circumcised. Three days later, while all of them were still in pain, two of Jacob's sons, Simeon and Levi, Dinah's brothers, took their swords and attacked the unsuspecting city, killing every male. They put Hamor and his son Shechem to the sword and took Dinah from Shechem's house and left. The sons of Jacob came upon the dead bodies and looted the city where their sister had been defiled. They seized their flocks and herds and donkeys and everything else of theirs in the city and out in the fields. They carried off all their wealth and all their women and children, taking as plunder everything in the houses.

Then Jacob said to Simeon and Levi, "You have brought trouble on me by making me a stench to the Canaanites and Perizzites, the people living in this land. We are few in number, and if they join forces against me and attack me, I and my household will be destroyed." But they replied, "Should he have treated our sister like a prostitute?"

UNDERSTANDING:

1. What was Jacob's sin in regard to his daughter?
2. What happened to Dinah as a result?
3. How did this cause her brothers to sin?

WISDOM:

What biblical principle did Jacob ignore when he allowed Dinah to have friends in the land?

NOTES

WEEK SIX—DAY FOUR

Intermarriage

KNOWLEDGE:

Nehemiah 13:23-27

Moreover, in those days I saw men of Judah who had married women from Ashdod, Ammon and Moab. Half of their children spoke the language of Ashdod or the language of one of the other peoples, and did not know how to speak the language of Judah. I rebuked them and called curses down on them. I beat some of the men and pulled out their hair. I made them take an oath in God's name and said: "You are not to give your daughters in marriage to their sons, nor are you to take their daughters in marriage for your sons or for yourselves. Was it not because of marriages like these that Solomon king of Israel sinned? Among the many nations there was no king like him. He was loved by his God, and God made him king over all Israel, but even he was led into sin by foreign women. Must we hear now that you too are doing all this terrible wickedness and are being unfaithful to our God by marrying foreign women?"

Ezra 10:1-4

While Ezra was praying and confessing, weeping and throwing himself down before the house of God, a large crowd of Israelites—men, women and children—gathered around him. They too wept bitterly. Then Shecaniah son of Jehiel, one of the descendants of Elam, said to Ezra, "We have been unfaithful to our God by marrying foreign women from the peoples around us. But in spite of this, there is still hope for Israel. Now let us make a covenant before our God to send away all these women and their children, in accordance with the counsel of my LORD and of those who fear the commands of our God. Let it be done according to the Law. Rise up; this matter is in your hands. We will support you, so take courage and do it."

Ezra 10:9-11,18

Within the three days, all the men of Judah and Benjamin had gathered in Jerusalem. And on the twentieth day of the ninth month, all the people were sitting in the square before the house of God, greatly distressed by the occasion and because of the rain. Then Ezra the priest stood up and said to them, "You have been unfaithful; you have married foreign women, adding to Israel's guilt. Now make confession to the LORD, the God of your fathers, and do his will. Separate yourselves from the peoples around you and from your foreign wives." (They all gave their hands in pledge to put away their wives, and for their guilt they each presented a ram from the flock as a guilt offering.)

UNDERSTANDING:

1. What was the result of Israelites intermingling with foreigners?
2. What did it cost them later?

WISDOM:

James 4:4 says "Don't you know that friendship with the world is hatred toward God? Anyone who chooses to be a friend of the world becomes an enemy of God." What is the ever-present danger in flirting with the world?

NOTES

WEEK SIX—DAY FIVE

Companions

KNOWLEDGE:

Proverbs 12:26

A righteous man is cautious in friendship,
but the way of the wicked leads them astray.

Proverbs 13:20

He who walks with the wise grows wise,
but a companion of fools suffers harm.

Proverbs 14:7

Stay away from a foolish man,
for you will not find knowledge on his lips.

Proverbs 22:5

In the paths of the wicked lie thorns and snares,
but he who guards his soul stays far from them.

Proverbs 24:1-2

Do not envy wicked men,
do not desire their company;

for their hearts plot violence,
and their lips talk about making trouble.

1 Corinthians 15:33

Do not be misled: "Bad company corrupts good character."

UNDERSTANDING:

1. What does Solomon continually warn us about?
2. What is the responsibility of parents for their children in this regard?

WISDOM:

What are the biblical principles in these verses and how can we apply these principles in making a decision about where to send children to school?

NOTES

Chapter 7

The Art of Deception

See to it that no one takes you captive through hollow and deceptive philosophy, which depends on human tradition and the basic principles of this world rather than on Christ.

—Colossians 2:8

TRUTH IS SO important to God that the prohibition of speaking falsely is one of the Ten Commandments. Truth is so important to God that Jesus declared he was born "to testify to the truth" (John 18:37). In fact, Jesus claimed to *be* the truth. God detests falsehood. David writes in the Psalms, "I hate and abhor falsehood, but I love your law" (Psalm 119:163). David had great insight into the heart of God. He felt what God felt; what God called good, David called good, and what God called evil, David called evil. David was a man after God's own heart. Centuries after David's reign, God told Isaiah, "my people will go into exile for lack of understanding...woe to those who call evil good and good evil" (Isaiah 5:13,20). Those who call evil good and good evil are liars, and lies of any kind, even lies of omission, are an abomination to God, because lies take people captive.

It is no small matter then, when children are lied to in the classroom. No parents would willingly leave their child in the care of a teacher if they suspected any wrongdoing on the teacher's part. Yet many parents entrust their children to teachers who are teaching counterfeit knowledge. It is no doubt true that the majority of teachers, especially if they are Christians, have no idea at all that they are disseminating lies in the classroom, and would be dismayed to know the truth. The problem is that the teachers themselves have been indoctrinated in the lies of the culture and they pass those beliefs along in the classroom. *Teacher indoctrination is the whole point of State certification.* Remember, ninety-one percent of evangelical Christians do not have a biblical worldview. Teachers are no exception. And teachers pass their worldviews on to their students. Jesus said, "A student is not above his teacher, but everyone who is well-trained will be like his teacher" (Luke 6:40). Both parents and teachers will be held accountable to God for any deception that takes place in the classroom.

Deception in the classroom usually takes one of three forms: 1) outright lies, such as teaching evolutionary origin of life or teaching that sexual activity should be free of moral constraint; 2) lies of omission, such as teaching a revision of history by removing all traces of Christianity from the classroom; and 3) the use of deceptive methodology, which can literally incapacitate a child in his ability to think logically.

The first form is so obvious, it needs no discussion here. The second form is harder to detect, especially if parents themselves have studied revised history. This will be discussed only briefly since other books have been written on this topic. It is the third form of deception, the methodology, which needs more attention, because if the methodology is effective, students will lose their ability to think clearly, and will no longer be able to discern the truth from a lie.

It is no secret that history has been completely rewritten from the politically correct viewpoint. Check out any social studies, world history, civics, or U.S. history book from your local school. If you went to school in the 1950's or 1960's, you may not recognize your own history. Nearly every reference to God has been removed, and Christianity itself is either ridiculed or portrayed as a religion of greed and intolerance. Original documents have been edited. The Mayflower Compact, the Declaration of Independence, and original State documents have all had any mention of Christianity removed. Our founding fathers are pejoratively referred to as Deists who designed our system of government on the Enlightenment ideas of pre-revolutionary France, rather than on the biblical principles derived from Scripture. Frequently, history is shown from the viewpoint of our national enemies, giving students a decidedly anti-American bias. Capitalism is denounced, and socialist propaganda is infused into nearly every subject, including math.

Schools in some districts are not willing to allow parents to take their children's textbooks home for review, making it difficult for parents to evaluate the texts. Michael J. Chapman, author of *Dreamers of a Godless Utopia: How to Recognize Worldview Bias in Education,* has researched many of the most popular textbooks used in schools today, in both primary and secondary schools. He reviews each of the texts, and gives examples from each text in his book. He evaluates not only the content, but the methodology used in the books. Every parent who has children in school should read this book whether they are Christian or not. Regardless of religious persuasion, parents need to know what their children are taught in school.

Most Christian parents who send their children to public schools are aware that their children will be given some false information, but they believe they can counteract any false teachings their kids pick up at school. What parents do not realize is that children who are exposed to two competing worldviews are in more danger of losing their ability to think clearly and evaluate truth than children who are trained in only one worldview. The system specifically targets any child who comes to school with values and a worldview that are incompatible with the worldview of the State. The enemy is clever; he uses us to do his work.

If you were to visit a modern-day classroom, it would probably look very much like the classrooms we all grew up in. You would never know from mere observation that these classrooms are the front lines of the great cosmic battle. This is the place where worldviews converge and engage in mortal combat. The techniques and methodologies that are used to capture the minds of the children are so diabolical that unless a parent really knows what to look for, he will miss it even if he scrupulously reads the textbooks. In fact, these techniques are designed so that even the teachers who employ them have no idea how the process is damaging the minds of their charges.

In chapter 3, the Hegelian dialectic was introduced as a technique developed by the Prussian philosopher Georg Wilhelm Friedrich Hegel. Hegel was a man who deified the State, an atheist who promoted State ownership of its citizens. He did not believe in absolute truth, but believed that truth evolved over time. The dialectic he devised works like this: For every truth claim (thesis) there is an opposing truth claim (antithesis). If we take both truth claims and put them together, we come up with a new truth claim (synthesis). This is done by group consensus through dialogue. The new truth claim is then set up against another opposing truth claim, and a new truth evolves from the synthesis of these two. Truth is always evolving, always determined by the group.

On the surface, Hegel's dialectic might seem appealing. It certainly appeals to our politically correct culture today. We often hear, "You have your truth, I have mine. We will all be tolerant of each other and get along." Or we hear that every religion has some truth; each leads to God, but in a different way. This kind of thinking is dangerous, because if we believe we can accept two contradictory statements as each partially true, then we subconsciously accept the premise that there is no absolute truth. If we accept the premise that there is no absolute truth, we have just ruled out the possibility of the existence of God. Furthermore, when we allow our minds to embrace a contradiction, we are disabling the mechanism in our brains that enables us to think clearly.

Hegel's technique for determining truth flies in the face of simple logic. Suppose we have truth claim (A) and its opposite (B). We can say A is (not B) and B is (not A). A is the thesis and B is the antithesis. According to the rules of logic, every statement is either true or false, and can be tested in a number of ways to determine its truth. We can say this because we define truth as that which corresponds to reality as perceived by God. A statement either corresponds to that reality or it doesn't. Therefore, a statement is either true or not true. Let us say that A is true. Then B is (not A), therefore not true. A and B are mutually exclusive and therefore cannot be synthesized. There is no common ground.

Logic, like mathematics, is a tool given to us by our Creator so that we can understand our world, discern truth from lies, and have the ability to reason. Reason separates man from the animals. God made us in his image so we could have a relationship with him. "Come, let us reason together," he says in Isaiah (Isaiah 1:18). The human mind cannot wrap itself around logical contradictions without warping the mind. Once a child wraps his mind around a logical contradiction, he can be made to believe anything, no matter how absurd. Voltaire once said, "Anyone who has the power to make you believe absurdities has the power to make you commit atrocities."[39] Many Christian kids were part of Hitler Youth. This is precisely why indoctrination into two worldviews is so extremely dangerous for Christian children. When we expose our children to one truth at home and another "truth" at school, we are unwittingly contributing to the destruction of their minds.

The strategies of the Hegelian dialectic were developed in Germany and the UK. They were then fine-tuned in America at places like Harvard, Stanford, and Columbia, with the specific intent of adapting the dialectic to children.[40] Other names for the Hegelian dialectic which you may recognize are outcome-based education, values clarification, behavior modification, higher order thinking skills, cooperative learning, the Delphi technique, dialoguing to consensus, critical thinking, or synthesis. Behavioral scientists are part of the teams who write the textbooks our children use at school. The textbooks are specifically designed to change the thoughts, feelings, and behaviors of the students. Here is how it works:

A child of five, six, or seven is exposed to new ideas at school. At this age, no child has the experience or the mental ability to effectively challenge what is taught. They trust their teachers implicitly while the groundwork is laid. "Cooperation" is stressed, day in and day out. By the time a child is ten or twelve, she is beginning to realize that some things do not make sense, but the teacher and the other students all seem to agree. In order to be accepted as part of the group, she agrees also, perhaps reluctantly at first. After all, she has learned from kindergarten on up that consensus is more important than principle.

The dialectic process most often takes the form of asking open-ended questions. The exercises are designed to enforce the idea that there is no right or wrong answer. Everyone has a right to his opinion and no one has the right to say his answer is the correct one. In other words, there are no absolutes and everything is relative. Once the children understand this, the teacher can move forward to help children arrive at the "proper" answers through group consensus.

In one popular fifth-grade social studies textbook,[41] the section called Points of View operates in this way: The question is, "Should we celebrate Columbus Day?" The textbook itself gives no information about Christopher Columbus. Instead, three opinions are offered to the children, two of which are written by college professors. The two professors are Native Americans who charge Columbus with destroying a nation and a culture. The third person, from the Italian-American service organization, writes a paragraph about Columbus, about his courage and sense of adventure and curiosity. In the discussion, students are reminded that the professors are experts in the field of studying people and their cultures. The children are then asked to make "their own" decision. The job of the teacher is to make sure the group reaches the (politically) correct answer.

Wait a minute. We thought there were no correct answers. However, teachers are expected to teach certain values to their students. Here is a seven-point list of values given to teachers in North Carolina at an in-service workshop:[42]

1. There is no right and wrong, only conditioned responses.
2. The collective good is more important than the individual.
3. Consensus is more important than principle.

4. Flexibility is more important than accomplishment.
5. Nothing is permanent except change.
6. All ethics are situational; there are no moral absolutes.
7. There are no perpetrators, only victims.

These workshops are given in every state, usually under the guise of diversity training. Consensus and cooperation are the bedrock of global training and the Hegelian dialectic is the cornerstone of global education.

The child who is a Christian has her beliefs challenged in class day after day after day, and does not even realize it. No one says anything about God or Jesus or Christianity. But as she slowly acquiesces to the pressure of conforming to the group consensus, she is losing her belief in absolute truth and in her right to defend it. A psychological conflict is set up in the child's mind, resulting from indoctrination in two worldviews. The term psychologists use for this conflict is *cognitive dissonance.* This is a psychological condition that leaves a child morally disoriented and defenseless, because the only way to resolve the tension it creates is to succumb to acceptance of contradictory beliefs. When a child crosses this line, she can no longer accept any kind of belief in absolute truth. Sean McDowell testifies to the confusion of our Protestant youth in an article he wrote for the *Christian Research Journal.* He says, "Recent studies reveal that the majority of our youth (81 percent) have adopted the view that 'all truth is relative to the individual and his/her circumstances.'"[43]

Teachers are frequently not aware of the damage they are doing to students because the techniques that are used are hidden even from them. Michael J. Chapman gives a perfect analogy to how the Hegelian dialectic is employed to draw students into the worldview of secular humanism. He writes,

...It is the art of propaganda through language manipulation, omission of fact, censorship, and selective story telling in order to present a distorted or biased understanding of reality.

Consider the analogy of an artist mixing color for his overall painting. The artist is a propagandist, and he is painting Humanism, which is green in color. If the artist simply used green paint, everyone would see green and the propaganda would be easily exposed. However, just as the impressionists discovered, a clever propagandist can achieve a much more vibrant and powerful green by placing single brush strokes of yellow next to strokes of blue, then allowing the *viewer's eye* to do the mixing. If you look too closely at the painting, you will see only the harmless strokes of yellow and blue; but step back and open your eyes to the entire painting and a vibrant deep green will appear...

We tend to see the painting in bits and pieces only. Each educator is trained to unwittingly apply a single brush stroke of blue or yellow onto the canvas. Each stroke is a nice sounding story, colorful illustration, or a delightful experience; but the image it finally creates in the mind of children is the world of secular humanism.[44]

It would be far too easy to simply put the blame on teachers for what our children are learning in school. Many of the teachers themselves have believed the lies of our culture and do not realize that they are teaching lies. That does not let them off the hook, but it does lessen the degree of guilt. There are many Christian teachers out there who are aware of the situation and who are bucking the system by managing their own classrooms and not using the textbooks that are issued to them. They have to design their own lesson plans, but they are up to the task. Thank God for them. They refuse to be intimidated, and they are risking their careers to do the right thing.

Training the mind of a child is the most important job parents have. Protecting the mind is far more important than protecting the body. When the child's mind is destroyed, eternity hangs in the balance. We are given warning after warning in Scripture about the consequences of suppressing the truth and believing lies. Romans chapter one says, "The wrath of God is being revealed from heaven against all the godlessness and wickedness of men who suppress the truth...for although they knew God, they neither glorified him as God nor gave thanks to him, *but their thinking became futile and their foolish hearts were darkened... Furthermore, since they did not think it worthwhile to retain the knowledge of God, he gave them over to a depraved mind."*

Paul emphasizes this again in his letter to the Ephesians when he says, "So I tell you this and insist on it in the Lord, that you must no longer live as the Gentiles do, *in the futility of their thinking. They are darkened in their understanding* and separated from the life of God because of the ignorance that is in them due to the hardening of their hearts" (Ephesians 4:17-18). The Hegelian dialectic is a perfect example of the "futility of their thinking." God forbid that our children slip into this way of thinking.

The Scripture at the beginning of this chapter bears repeating. *"See to it that no one takes you captive through hollow and deceptive philosophy, which depends on human tradition and the basic principles of this world rather than on Christ."* Every sin we commit can be traced back to belief in a lie. It is never too late to turn around. Scripture assures us that we can (and must!) be transformed by the renewing of our minds. But there is a catch: *"Do not conform any longer to the pattern of this world,* but be transformed by the renewing of your mind. Then you will be able to test and approve what God's will is—his good, pleasing and perfect will." Transformation is possible, but only if we obey.

Soli Deo Gloria

FURTHER UP
AND
FURTHER IN

WEEK SEVEN—DAY ONE

Remember

KNOWLEDGE:

Numbers 15:39-40

You will have these tassels to look at and so you will remember all the commands of the LORD, that you may obey them and not prostitute yourselves by going after the lusts of your own hearts and eyes. Then you will remember to obey all my commands and will be consecrated to your God.

Deuteronomy 6:6-9

These commandments that I give you today are to be upon your hearts. Impress them on your children. Talk about them when you sit at home and when you walk along the road, when you lie down and when you get up. Tie them as symbols on your hands and bind them on your foreheads.

Deuteronomy 9:7

Remember this and never forget how you provoked the LORD your God to anger in the desert. From the day you left Egypt until you arrived here, you have been rebellious against the LORD.

Psalm 77:11

I will remember the deeds of the LORD; yes, I will remember your miracles of long ago.

Malachi 4:4

Remember the law of my servant Moses, the decrees and laws I gave him at Horeb for all Israel.

John 15:20

Remember the words I spoke to you: "No servant is greater than his master." If they persecuted me, they will persecute you also. If they obeyed my teaching, they will obey yours also.

Hebrews 10:32

Remember those earlier days after you had received the light, when you stood your ground in a great contest in the face of suffering.

Revelation 3:3

Remember, therefore, what you have received and heard; obey it, and repent. But if you do not wake up, I will come like a thief, and you will not know at what time I will come to you.

UNDERSTANDING:

1. How important is it to know history?
2. List all the things we are to remember.
3. What are parents instructed to do?

WISDOM:

1. According to Revelation 3:3, what are we supposed to do after we remember?
2. From what do you need to repent?

NOTES

Week Seven—Day Two

Disobedience

KNOWLEDGE:

Deuteronomy 11

Love the LORD your God and keep his requirements, his decrees, his laws and his commands always. Remember today that your children were not the ones who saw and experienced the discipline of the LORD your God: his majesty, his mighty hand, his outstretched arm; the signs he performed and the things he did in the heart of Egypt, both to Pharaoh king of Egypt and to his whole country; what he did to the Egyptian army, to its horses and chariots, how he overwhelmed them with the waters of the Red Sea as they were pursuing you, and how the LORD brought lasting ruin on them. It was not your children who saw what he did for you in the desert until you arrived at this place, and what he did to Dathan and Abiram, sons of Eliab the Reubenite, when the earth opened its mouth right in the middle of all Israel and swallowed them up with their households, their tents and every living thing that belonged to them. But it was your own eyes that saw all these great things the LORD has done.

Observe therefore all the commands I am giving you today, so that you may have the strength to go in and take over the land that you are crossing the Jordan to possess, and so that you may live long in the land that the LORD swore to your forefathers to give to them and their descendants, a land flowing with milk and honey. The land you are entering to take over is not like the land of Egypt, from which you have come, where you planted your seed and irrigated it by foot as in a vegetable garden. But the land you are crossing the Jordan to take possession of is a land of mountains and valleys that drinks rain from heaven. It is a land the LORD your God cares for; the eyes of the LORD your God are continually on it from the beginning of the year to its end.

So if you faithfully obey the commands I am giving you today—to love the LORD your God and to serve him with all your heart and with all your soul—then I will send rain on your land in its season, both autumn and spring rains, so that you may gather in your grain, new wine and oil. I will provide grass in the fields for your cattle, and you will eat and be satisfied.

Be careful, or you will be enticed to turn away and worship other gods and bow down to them. Then the LORD's anger will burn against you, and he will shut the heavens so that it will not rain and the ground will yield no produce, and you will soon perish from the good land the LORD is giving you. Fix these words of mine in your hearts and minds; tie them as symbols on your hands and bind them on your foreheads. Teach them to your children, talking about them when you sit at home and when you walk along the road, when you lie down and when you get up. Write them on the doorframes of your houses and on your gates, so that your days and the days of your children may be many in the land that the LORD swore to give your forefathers, as many as the days that the heavens are above the earth.

Judges 2:10-13

After that whole generation had been gathered to their fathers, another generation grew up, who knew neither the LORD nor what he had done for Israel. Then the Israelites did evil in the eyes of the LORD and served the Baals. They forsook the LORD, the God of their fathers, who had brought them out of Egypt. They followed and worshipped various gods of the peoples around them. They provoked the LORD to anger because they forsook him and served Baal and the Ashtoreths.

UNDERSTANDING:

1. Did the Israelites do as God had commanded them?
2. What happened to their children?

WISDOM:

1. Were the consequences for their children temporary or eternal?
2. What should we learn from this?

NOTES

WEEK SEVEN—DAY THREE

Historical Revisionism

KNOWLEDGE:

Genesis 3:1-5

Now the serpent was more crafty than any of the wild animals the LORD God had made. He said to the woman, "Did God really say, 'You must not eat from any tree in the garden'?" The woman said to the serpent, "We may eat fruit from the trees in the garden, but God did say, 'You must not eat fruit from the tree that is in the middle of the garden, and you must not touch it, or you will die.'" "You will not surely die," the serpent said to the woman. "For God knows that when you eat of it your eyes will be opened, and you will be like God, knowing good and evil."

1 Kings 12:26-28

Jeroboam thought to himself, "The kingdom will now likely revert to the house of David. If these people go up to offer sacrifices at the temple of the LORD in Jerusalem, they will again give their allegiance to their LORD, Rehoboam king of Judah. They will kill me and return to King Rehoboam." After seeking advice, the king made two golden calves. He said to the people, "It is too much for you to go up to Jerusalem. Here are your gods, O Israel, who brought you up out of Egypt."

Matthew 28:11-15

While the women were on their way, some of the guards went into the city and reported to the chief priests everything that had happened. When the chief priests had met with the elders and devised a plan, they gave the soldiers a large sum of money, telling them, "You are to say, 'His disciples came during the night and stole him away while we were asleep.' If this report gets to the governor, we will satisfy him and keep you out of trouble." So the soldiers took the money and did as they were instructed. And this story has been widely circulated among the Jews to this very day.

UNDERSTANDING:

Show how each of the above stories is an example of historical revisionism. What were the consequences for all who believed the revised history?

WISDOM:

What is the ultimate danger when our children are taught a revised history at school with all mention of God removed from the curriculum?

NOTES

Week Seven—Day Four

Logical Thinking

KNOWLEDGE:

Isaiah 1:18

"Come now, let us reason together," says the LORD. "Though your sins are like scarlet, they shall be as white as snow; though they are red as crimson, they shall be like wool."

1 Corinthians 6:9-10

Do you not know that the wicked will not inherit the kingdom of God? Do not be deceived: Neither the sexually immoral nor idolaters nor adulterers nor male prostitutes nor homosexual offenders nor thieves nor the greedy nor drunkards nor slanderers nor swindlers will inherit the kingdom of God.

1 Corinthians 15:33 (ESV)

Do not be deceived: "Bad company ruins good morals."

Galatians 6:7

Do not be deceived: God cannot be mocked. A man reaps what he sows.

James 1:16-18

Don't be deceived, my dear brothers. Every good and perfect gift is from above, coming down from the Father of the heavenly lights, who does not change like shifting shadows. He chose to give us birth through the word of truth, that we might be a kind of firstfruits of all he created.

Colossians 2:4

I tell you this so that no one may deceive you by fine-sounding arguments...See to it that no one takes you captive through hollow and deceptive philosophy, which depends on human tradition and the basic principles of this world rather than on Christ.

Ephesians 4:17-18

So I tell you this, and insist on it in the Lord, that you must no longer live as the Gentiles do, in the futility of their thinking. They are darkened in their understanding and separated from the life of God because of the ignorance that is in them due to the hardening of their hearts.

1 Peter 4:7

The end of all things is near. Therefore be clear minded and self-controlled so that you can pray.

Romans 1:28

Furthermore, since they did not think it worthwhile to retain the knowledge of God, he gave them over to a depraved mind, to do what ought not to be done.

2 Corinthians 10:5

We demolish arguments and every pretension that sets itself up against the knowledge of God, and we take captive every thought to make it obedient to Christ.

UNDERSTANDING:

1. Why is it very important that Christians be able to think clearly?
2. What things should we not be deceived about?
3. What does God want us to do according to Isaiah 1:18?

4. What are the consequences of being deceived?

WISDOM:

1. How does the Hegelian Dialectic prevent us from thinking logically?
2. How does Paul describe the way the world thinks in Ephesians 4:17-18 and in Romans 1:28?
3. Is it possible to carry out the command of 2 Corinthians 10:5 if we think like the world thinks?

NOTES

Two Trees of Knowledge

WEEK SEVEN—DAY FIVE

Those Who Tell Lies

KNOWLEDGE:

Psalm 5

For the director of music. For flutes. A psalm of David.
1 Give ear to my words, O LORD,
consider my sighing.

2 Listen to my cry for help,
    my King and my God,
    for to you I pray.

3 In the morning, O LORD, you hear my voice;
    in the morning I lay my requests before you
    and wait in expectation.

4 You are not a God who takes pleasure in evil;
    with you the wicked cannot dwell.

5 The arrogant cannot stand in your presence;
    you hate all who do wrong.

6 You destroy those who tell lies;
    bloodthirsty and deceitful men
    the LORD abhors.

7 But I, by your great mercy,
    will come into your house;
    in reverence will I bow down
    toward your holy temple.

8 Lead me, O LORD, in your righteousness
  because of my enemies—
  make straight your way before me.

9 Not a word from their mouth can be trusted;
  their heart is filled with destruction.
  Their throat is an open grave;
  with their tongue they speak deceit.

10 Declare them guilty, O God!
  Let their intrigues be their downfall.
  Banish them for their many sins,
  for they have rebelled against you.

11 But let all who take refuge in you be glad;
  let them ever sing for joy.
  Spread your protection over them,
  that those who love your name may rejoice in you.

12 For surely, O LORD, you bless the righteous;
  you surround them with your favor as with a shield.

UNDERSTANDING:

1. Whom does God abhor?
2. What does he do to those who lie?

WISDOM:

Does God make exceptions for people who are unaware that they are lying?

NOTES

_____

_____

_____

_____

_____

_____

_____

_____

_____

_____

_____

_____

Chapter 8

Fit for Heaven

Your kingdom come, your will be done on earth as it is in heaven.
—Matthew 6:10

ACCORDING TO THE State, the purpose of education is to produce citizens who will serve the State. The citizen who best serves the State is one who values consensus and cooperation and who follows orders without asking questions. The State's focus is on the corporate body of students—hence standardized testing and class assignment based on age. The eye of the State is continually on the global community, and its goal is to build a global economy.

> *This present age is only a temporary intrusion in the perfect world that God created... True education, therefore, must be education that will equip people for fruitful lives in both time and eternity.*
> —Henry M. Morris

According to Scripture, the purpose of education is to train students to do the things for which God has wired them: "For we are God's workmanship created in Christ Jesus to do good works, which God prepared in advance for us to do"

(Ephesians 2:10). Proverbs 22:6 advises us to "train up a child in the way he should go." A careful study of this verse reveals that the word "he" is significant. The education of each child is individualized according to the way *that child* should go—according to *his bent*. It is up to the parent to study each child, and to the best of their ability train that child for the specific work God has prepared in advance for him, which will be the work he does for all eternity.

In God's view, this present world is merely the training ground for the real life we will experience on the new earth. "And he made known to us the mystery of his will according to his good pleasure, which he purposed in Christ, *to be put into effect when the times will have reached their fulfillment—to bring all things in heaven and on earth together under one head, even Christ*" (Ephesians 1:9). When Jesus prayed, "Your kingdom come, your will be done on earth as it is in heaven," he was giving us a blueprint for the task we have on this earth—to transform our culture by living according to the design that God put into effect at Creation. This design is eternal; it is the design that will be perfectly practiced on the new earth. It is the design that is already practiced in heaven, because it flows forth from the very nature of God. Our goal as parents should be to give our children an education that will fit them for heaven, not for Harvard.

Today, however, we find ourselves in a metaphysical dilemma. We do not think much about heaven, and if we do think of it at all, it doesn't seem real to us. This present world has become our reality. We've all said it from time to time. We graduate from school, and it's out to the "real world" that we go. We attend church on Sunday, and then on Monday it's back to the "real world." Our words imply that the world we inhabit on Sunday is not the real world. It's merely a retreat from the "real world." We believe heaven is a spiritual place where God lives and we will someday live, but our life work, our careers, are for this present world. If this is true, then all of our education will be geared to learning how to succeed in this world. Our focus will be on learning how the world works *from the world's point of view.* This has an unfortunate impact on the way we live and the way we train our children.

In the history of Christendom, this is a new way of thinking. Throughout Scripture, from Adam through the apostles, God's people believed that this present world was merely a shadow of the real thing. C.S. Lewis called this world the "shadowlands." The real world, the place God inhabits and is preparing for us, is the one saints throughout history have put their hope in. Hebrews 11 makes this clear. After giving us a list of saints in the "hall of faith," the writer of Hebrews says this,

> All these people were still living by faith when they died. They did not receive the things promised; they only saw them and welcomed them from a distance. And they admitted that they were aliens and strangers on earth. People who say such things show that they are looking for a country of their own. If they had been thinking of the country they had left, they would have had opportunity to return. Instead, they were longing for a better country—a heavenly one. Therefore God is not ashamed to be called their God, for he has prepared a city for them.
> —Hebrews 11:13-16

The world God is preparing for us is the real world. Moses and the others mentioned in Hebrews 11 knew this. Moses "left Egypt, not fearing the king's anger, he persevered because he saw him who is invisible." Moses could do this because he was "looking ahead to his reward." His reward was not the land of Canaan. Moses never entered the land of Canaan. His reward was the real Promised Land—the land all of God's people will inhabit when we die. Hebrews 11 ends with this verse: "These were all commended for their faith, yet none of them received what had been promised. God planned something better for us so that only together with us would they be made perfect."

Part of the reason Christians no longer believe that the future world is the real one is that we have been brainwashed into believing that nothing exists if it does not exist empirically. In other words, if we can't see it, smell it, feel it, touch it, and perform experiments on it, it isn't real. Our ideas of heaven are warped; most of us never give it a second thought. We have come to believe that heaven is a spiritual place where our souls will forever be caught up in an eternal worship service, where every day is Sunday and all our earthly pleasures will be gone for good. No wonder we do not look forward to it. In order to better understand what it is we are to train our children for, we need to digress for a bit to study what Scripture tells us about our future home.

Scripture gives us many clues to what heaven will be like, but you won't find a book of the Bible dedicated to this topic. Instead, these little jewels are scattered throughout the Scriptures, mostly in the Old Testament prophets. Perhaps God has deliberately hidden heaven in the pages of Scripture so we could enjoy the thrill of a treasure hunt. Imagine his delight as we unearth these unexpected treasures and store them up in our hearts. The problem is, the Old Testament prophets do not appear on the *New York Times* bestseller list. We do not study them and mine the precious jewels that are free for the seeking. Besides, we believe that thoughts of heaven will distract us from our work here. We think our work here is the primary thing, and heaven is just a spiritual retirement package. We may even convince ourselves that it is wrong to think about heaven all the time because as Christians we aren't supposed to be thinking about what's in it for us.

Many Christians might be surprised to learn that God has commanded us to think about heaven all the time. Everything we do on this earth should be motivated by our rewards in heaven. We've already seen that the Old Testament saints were motivated by their rewards in heaven. According to Hebrews 11, God commended them for their exemplary faith in his promises. In Colossians 3 Paul writes, "Since, then, you have been raised with Christ, *set your hearts on things above*, where Christ is seated at the right hand of God. *Set your minds on things above, not on earthly things*" (verses 1-2). This is exactly opposite of what many think we are supposed to do. Yet Hebrews 12 points out that this is just what Jesus did: "Let us fix our eyes on Jesus, the author and perfecter of our faith, *who for the joy set before him* endured the cross, scorning its shame, and sat down at the right hand of the throne of God" (verse 2).

Jesus did what he did for the joy set before him. What joy? Wasn't he already in heaven with God before he came here? Was he missing something there that he should come here and suffer? Yes! We were not there with him. We are the bride that the Father presented to his Son before the foundations of this world were laid. He loved us with an undying love. When we were taken captive by the prince of this world, there was no rest in heaven. Jesus came to earth to ransom his bride so we could live with him forever. He came here to woo us to himself the way a lover woos the beloved. Jesus offers his bride rewards and treasures just the way a lover offers treasures to his beloved. He wants us to delight in these treasures.

In the beatitudes (Matthew 5:3-12), Christ offers us the earth and the kingdom of heaven! The treasures he offers us are not for this present world, but for the next. He says, "Do not store up treasures for yourselves on earth...but store up for yourselves treasures in heaven...for where your treasure is, there will your heart be also" (Matthew 6:19-21). He adds, "But seek ye first his kingdom and his righteousness, and all these things will be given you as well" (Matthew 6:33). "Ask and it will be given you, seek and you will find, knock and the door will be opened to you" (Matthew 7:7). "If you, then, though you are evil, know how to give good gifts to your children, how much more will your Father in heaven give good gifts to those who ask him!" (Matthew 7:11). How did we ever come to believe that desiring rewards is wrong?

God calls us to focus our lives on heaven. He wants us to evaluate every thought, every word, every action in light of our eternal reward. Paul warns us that "the fire will test the quality of each man's work. If what he has built survives, he will receive his reward. If it is burned up, he will suffer loss" (1 Corinthians 3:13-14). If we had any idea what this meant, it would change our lives forever.

Scripture tells us that when we die, we will go to heaven to be with God. But that is only a temporary arrangement. After Christ returns,

God will destroy this present cosmos and create a new earth and new heavens. We will be reunited with our glorified bodies and will inhabit the new earth. The kingdom of heaven will then descend and become the dwelling place of God *on earth*. Yes, God will dwell with us on earth, not the other way around. *He will dwell in our natural habitat.* That is what Immanuel means, "God with us."

We will be fully human with human flesh and blood and bones. For the first time in our lives we will reach our full potential as human beings, uninhibited by sin, corruption, disease, or deficiency. We will be fully recognizable in glorified bodies that will never run down. We will have human appetites for food and work and adventure. The work we are given to do will be the work for which we were born—(the kind of jobs we feel guilty getting paid for because we love them so much!) There will be feasts and festivals and games and parades. There will be a wedding, the likes of which we have never seen on this present earth.

For the first time in the history of the world, we will perfectly fulfill God's command to subdue the earth and have dominion over it. We will be in charge of animals and agriculture, research and development, oceanic exploits and exploration of space. We will own property and rule over cities and countries. We will mine natural resources and feed the world. We will export and import goods and trade with nations. We will be teachers and students, kings and queens, doctors and lawyers, mothers and fathers.

> *Every single thing we do in heaven will be an act of worship. And that is just the point—because every single thing we do on earth should be an act of worship.*

The New Jerusalem will have no need of sun or moon because it is the dwelling place of God and He will be its light. But the rest of the world will be run just as it always has, so we will not miss the stars and the campfires and the beautiful sunrises and sunsets. Jesus promises to "make all things new." "All things" means all things. That includes the new heavens with all of its stars and planets and galaxies. We may even be able to travel to far-away galaxies.

These descriptions are just glimpses of what God has promised us in the Scriptures.[45] They are just to whet our appetites. If you have never read the Bible in its entirety, now might be a good time to start this treasure hunt. See for yourself what God has promised to do for us. An eternal church service? No way! Every single thing we do in heaven will be an act of worship. And that is just the point—because every single thing we do on earth should be an act of worship. Farming is an act of worship for a farmer. Designing roads and buildings and websites are acts of worship for those who love to design stuff. Parenting is an act of worship within marriage. Teaching is an act of worship for teachers. In all of these things we bring glory to God and God alone, because we do the thing for which we have been created. *Soli Deo Gloria!*

Our job as parents is to train our children to do the things for which they were created—the things they will do, not only on this present earth, but for all eternity. We should not be so short-sighted that we train them only for success in this world with no thought of the next. Success in this world does not guarantee success in the next, but if our children are trained for heaven, they will be successful here as well. Paul makes this point in his first letter to Timothy: "If you point these things out to the brothers, you will be a good minister of Christ Jesus, brought up in the truths of the faith and of the good teaching that you have followed. Have nothing to do with godless myths and old wives' tales. Rather train yourself to be godly. For physical training is of some value, *but godliness has value for all things, holding promise for both the present life and the life to come*" (1 Timothy 4:6-8).

Those who are trained for the next world will be the most successful in the present world. This is because those who are trained in truth and righteousness know the truth about how this present world operates—not from the world's perspective, but from God's perspective. They know the underlying principles on which this world runs. Look at King David. David knew the heart of God like no other. A study of the Psalms proves that David understood how to live out the principles of God's Word. David's education must have been superb for him to be such a successful king. God himself was David's teacher. He taught David everything he needed to know in a sheep pen. "He chose David his servant and took him from the sheep pens; from tending the sheep he brought him to be the shepherd of his people Jacob, of Israel his inheritance. And David shepherded them with integrity of heart; with skillful hands he led them" (Psalm 78:70-72). David himself makes the following claim:

> Your commands make me wiser than my enemies, for they are ever with me. I have more insight than all my teachers, for I meditate on your statutes, I have more understanding than the elders, for I obey your precepts. I have kept my feet from every evil path so that I might obey your word. I have not departed from your laws for you yourself have taught me.
>
> —Psalm 119:98-102

David did not go to an accredited school for royal princes. God trained David for a job he will do for all eternity, and his training for heaven made him a success on earth.

Look at King Solomon. Scripture says "King Solomon was greater in riches and wisdom than all the other kings of the earth. All the kings of the earth sought audience with Solomon to hear the wisdom God had put in his heart. Year after year, everyone who came brought a gift—articles of silver and gold, and robes, weapons and spices, and horses and mules" (2 Chronicles 9:22-24). A study of the book of Proverbs reveals that Solomon learned everything he needed to know at the feet of his father, David. David was the one who trained Solomon and who repeatedly counseled his son to seek wisdom above all. It is no surprise then that when God appeared to Solomon and said to him, "Ask for whatever you want me to give you," Solomon asked for wisdom and knowledge. He asked for the things that have eternal value, and those things guaranteed his success in the temporal world.

When the Jews were taken into captivity, King Nebuchadnezzer ordered his chief official "to bring in some of the Israelites from the royal family and the nobility—young men without any physical defect, handsome, showing aptitude for every kind of learning, well informed, quick to understand, and qualified to serve in the king's palace." Daniel and his three friends were among them. These young men, however, resolved not to defile themselves at the king's table and were granted permission to be kept separate from the others. They did not get their training in wisdom from the State, either. Scripture records, "To these four young men, *God gave knowledge and understanding of all kinds of literature and learning...*In every matter of wisdom and understanding about which the king questioned them, he found them ten times better than all the magicians and enchanters in his whole kingdom" (see Daniel 1).

A Christian education is far superior to anything this world can provide, because it is based on biblical principles and truth. A Christian education views both worlds from God's perspective. God is the one who imparts knowledge in every area of life. He wants us to depend on him for our worldview, not on the world. Paul makes this clear in Romans 12: "Do not conform any longer to the pattern of this world, but be transformed *by the renewing of your mind.* Then you will be able to test and approve what God's will is—his good, pleasing and perfect will" (verse 2). Is a Christian education enough? "Do not deceive yourselves. If any one of you thinks he is wise by the standards of this age, he should become a "fool" so that he may become wise. For the wisdom of this world is foolishness in God's sight...The Lord knows that the thoughts of the wise are futile" (1 Corinthians 3:18-20). John Thomas McFarland wrote a child's prayer that expresses what a real education is supposed to do:

I love thee Lord Jesus, I ask thee to stay
Close by me forever and love me I pray

Two Trees of Knowledge

Bless all the dear children in thy tender care
And fit us for heaven to live with thee there.

God's refining fire will burn away all that cannot exist in heaven. Counterfeit knowledge will be burned up in that fire. A Christian education is the only education we can take with us.

Soli Deo Gloria

FURTHER UP
AND
FURTHER IN

Two Trees of Knowledge

WEEK EIGHT—DAY ONE

Fit for Heaven

KNOWLEDGE:

Isaiah 55

Invitation to the Thirsty
1 "Come, all you who are thirsty,
  come to the waters;
  and you who have no money,
  come, buy and eat!
  Come, buy wine and milk
  without money and without cost.

2 Why spend money on what is not bread,
  and your labor on what does not satisfy?
  Listen, listen to me, and eat what is good,
  and your soul will delight in the richest of fare.

3 Give ear and come to me;
  hear me, that your soul may live.
  I will make an everlasting covenant with you,
  my faithful love promised to David.

4 See, I have made him a witness to the peoples,
  a leader and commander of the peoples.

5 Surely you will summon nations you know not,
  and nations that do not know you will hasten to you,
  because of the LORD your God,
  the Holy One of Israel,
  for he has endowed you with splendor."

6 Seek the LORD while he may be found;
 call on him while he is near.

7 Let the wicked forsake his way
 and the evil man his thoughts.
 Let him turn to the LORD, and he will have mercy on him,
 and to our God, for he will freely pardon.

8 "For my thoughts are not your thoughts,
 neither are your ways my ways,"
 declares the LORD.

9 "As the heavens are higher than the earth,
 so are my ways higher than your ways
 and my thoughts than your thoughts.

10 As the rain and the snow
 come down from heaven,
 and do not return to it
 without watering the earth
 and making it bud and flourish,
 so that it yields seed for the sower and bread for the eater,

11 so is my word that goes out from my mouth:
 It will not return to me empty,
 but will accomplish what I desire
 and achieve the purpose for which I sent it.

12 You will go out in joy
 and be led forth in peace;
 the mountains and hills
 will burst into song before you,
 and all the trees of the field
 will clap their hands.

13 Instead of the thornbush will grow the pine tree,
and instead of briers the myrtle will grow.
This will be for the LORD's renown,
for an everlasting sign,
which will not be destroyed."

UNDERSTANDING:

1. In verses 1 and 2, what do the wine, milk, and bread symbolize?
2. How does knowledge affect the soul?
3. What does verse 6 imply, and why is it important that we begin our children's knowledge of God as soon as possible?
4. According to verse 11, what does true knowledge accomplish?
5. What indications do we have that this passage refers to life in heaven?

WISDOM:

Apply verses 2 and 9 to the concepts of the two trees of knowledge: counterfeit knowledge and knowledge of life. How do these verses speak to us about our choices for the education for God's children?

NOTES

_____

_____

_____

_____

_____

_____

_____

_____

_____

_____

_____

_____

_____

_____

WEEK EIGHT—DAY TWO

David

KNOWLEDGE:

Isaiah 54:13

All your sons will be taught by the LORD,
  and great will be your children's peace.

Psalm 78:70-72

He chose David his servant
  and took him from the sheep pens;
from tending the sheep he brought him
  to be the shepherd of his people Jacob,
  of Israel his inheritance.
And David shepherded them with integrity of heart;
  with skillful hands he led them.

Psalm 119:98-102

Your commands make me wiser than my enemies,
  for they are ever with me.
I have more insight than all my teachers,
  for I meditate on your statutes.
I have more understanding than the elders,
  for I obey your precepts.
I have kept my feet from every evil path
  so that I might obey your word.
I have not departed from your laws,
  for you yourself have taught me.

Ezekiel 37:24-28

"My servant David will be king over them, and they will all have one shepherd. They will follow my laws and be careful to keep my decrees. They will live in the land I gave to my servant Jacob, the land where your fathers lived. They and their children and their children's children will live there forever, and David my servant will be their prince forever. I will make a covenant of peace with them; it will be an everlasting covenant. I will establish them and increase their numbers, and I will put my sanctuary among them forever. My dwelling place will be with them; I will be their God, and they will be my people. Then the nations will know that I the LORD make Israel holy, when my sanctuary is among them forever."

Revelation 5:6-10

Then I saw a Lamb, looking as if it had been slain, standing in the center of the throne, encircled by the four living creatures and the elders. He had seven horns and seven eyes, which are the seven spirits of God sent out into all the earth. He came and took the scroll from the right hand of him who sat on the throne. And when he had taken it, the four living creatures and the twenty-four elders fell down before the Lamb. Each one had a harp and they were holding golden bowls full of incense, which are the prayers of the saints. And they sang a new song:

"You are worthy to take the scroll
and to open its seals,
because you were slain,
and with your blood you purchased men for God
from every tribe and language and people and nation.
You have made them to be a kingdom and priests to serve our God,
and they will reign on the earth."

UNDERSTANDING:

1. Who was David's teacher?
2. David did not receive the education normally given to aspiring kings. Did his education cripple him in any way?
3. The book of Ezekiel was written centuries after David's reign on earth. According to Ezekiel 37:24-28, was David's training designed for this temporal world only?

WISDOM:

Where will David reign in the future according to Ezekiel 37:24-28 and Revelation 5:10?

NOTES

_____

_____

_____

_____

_____

_____

_____

_____

_____

_____

_____

_____

_____

_____

WEEK EIGHT—DAY THREE

Solomon

KNOWLEDGE:

Proverbs 4

1 Listen, my sons, to a father's instruction;
  pay attention and gain understanding.
2 I give you sound learning,
  so do not forsake my teaching.
3 When I was a boy in my father's house,
  still tender, and an only child of my mother,
4 he taught me and said,
  "Lay hold of my words with all your heart;
  keep my commands and you will live."

1 Kings 4:29-34

God gave Solomon wisdom and very great insight, and a breadth of understanding as measureless as the sand on the seashore. Solomon's wisdom was greater than the wisdom of all the men of the East, and greater than all the wisdom of Egypt. He was wiser than any other man, including Ethan the Ezrahite—wiser than Heman, Calcol and Darda, the sons of Mahol. And his fame spread to all the surrounding nations. He spoke three thousand proverbs and his songs numbered a thousand and five. He described plant life, from the cedar of Lebanon to the hyssop that grows out of walls. He also taught about animals and birds, reptiles and fish. Men of all nations came to listen to Solomon's wisdom, sent by all the kings of the world, who had heard of his wisdom.

1 Kings 10:23-24

King Solomon was greater in riches and wisdom than all the other kings of the earth. The whole world sought audience with Solomon to hear the wisdom God had put in his heart.

2 Chronicles 9:22-24

King Solomon was greater in riches and wisdom than all the other kings of the earth. All the kings of the earth sought audience with Solomon to hear the wisdom God had put in his heart. Year after year, everyone who came brought a gift—articles of silver and gold, and robes, weapons and spices, and horses and mules.

UNDERSTANDING:

1. Who was Solomon's teacher according to Proverbs 4?
2. Who taught Solomon's sons?
3. Who gave Solomon wisdom?
4. What kinds of knowledge did God give to Solomon?
5. Was Solomon compromised in any way by missing out on a secular education?

WISDOM:

What is the relationship between parents being faithful to guard what has been entrusted to them and God giving wisdom to the children?

NOTES

_____

_____

_____

_____

_____

_____

_____

_____

_____

_____

_____

_____

_____

WEEK EIGHT—DAY FOUR

Daniel

KNOWLEDGE:

Daniel 1

Daniel's Training in Babylon

1 In the third year of the reign of Jehoiakim king of Judah, Nebuchadnezzar king of Babylon came to Jerusalem and besieged it. 2 And the LORD delivered Jehoiakim king of Judah into his hand, along with some of the articles from the temple of God. These he carried off to the temple of his god in Babylonia and put in the treasure house of his god.

3 Then the king ordered Ashpenaz, chief of his court officials, to bring in some of the Israelites from the royal family and the nobility- 4 young men without any physical defect, handsome, showing aptitude for every kind of learning, well informed, quick to understand, and qualified to serve in the king's palace. He was to teach them the language and literature of the Babylonians. 5 The king assigned them a daily amount of food and wine from the king's table. They were to be trained for three years, and after that they were to enter the king's service.

6 Among these were some from Judah: Daniel, Hananiah, Mishael and Azariah. 7 The chief official gave them new names: to Daniel, the name Belteshazzar; to Hananiah, Shadrach; to Mishael, Meshach; and to Azariah, Abednego.

8 But Daniel resolved not to defile himself with the royal food and wine, and he asked the chief official for permission not to defile himself this way. 9 Now God had caused the official to show favor and sympathy to Daniel, 10 but the official told Daniel, "I am afraid of my lord the king, who has assigned your food and drink. Why should he see you looking worse than the other young men your age? The king would then have my head because of you."

11 Daniel then said to the guard whom the chief official had appointed over Daniel, Hananiah, Mishael and Azariah, 12 "Please test your servants for ten days: Give us nothing but vegetables to eat and water to drink. 13 Then compare our appearance with that of the young men who eat the royal food, and treat your servants in accordance with what you see." 14 So he agreed to this and tested them for ten days.

15 At the end of the ten days they looked healthier and better nourished than any of the young men who ate the royal food. 16 So the guard took away their choice food and the wine they were to drink and gave them vegetables instead.

17 To these four young men God gave knowledge and understanding of all kinds of literature and learning. And Daniel could understand visions and dreams of all kinds.

18 At the end of the time set by the king to bring them in, the chief official presented them to Nebuchadnezzar. 19 The king talked with them, and he found none equal to Daniel, Hananiah, Mishael and Azariah; so they entered the king's service. 20 In every matter of wisdom and understanding about which the king questioned them, he found them ten times better than all the magicians and enchanters in his whole kingdom.

21 And Daniel remained there until the first year of King Cyrus.

UNDERSTANDING:

1. Why did Daniel and his friends refuse the king's food?
2. Were Daniel and his friends at a disadvantage because they relied on God alone?
3. What kinds of knowledge did God give to Daniel and his friends?

WISDOM:

1. What is the spiritual application of taking food from the State?

2. There were apparently many young men from the royal family in Israel who were brought into the king's service. Yet only these four from Judah refused the king's food. Do you think perhaps there is a relationship between their obedience in remaining undefiled (separate) and the wisdom imparted to them by God?

3. Does God give us wisdom just for the asking, or is there an obligation on our part?

NOTES

WEEK EIGHT—DAY FIVE

The Real World

KNOWLEDGE:

Hebrews 11:11-16; 32-40

By faith Abraham, even though he was past age—and Sarah herself was barren—was enabled to become a father because he considered him faithful who had made the promise. And so from this one man, and he as good as dead, came descendants as numerous as the stars in the sky and as countless as the sand on the seashore. All these people were still living by faith when they died. They did not receive the things promised; they only saw them and welcomed them from a distance. And they admitted that they were aliens and strangers on earth. People who say such things show that they are looking for a country of their own. If they had been thinking of the country they had left, they would have had opportunity to return. Instead, they were longing for a better country—a heavenly one. Therefore God is not ashamed to be called their God, for he has prepared a city for them.

And what more shall I say? I do not have time to tell about Gideon, Barak, Samson, Jephthah, David, Samuel and the prophets, who through faith conquered kingdoms, administered justice, and gained what was promised; who shut the mouths of lions, quenched the fury of the flames, and escaped the edge of the sword; whose weakness was turned to strength; and who became powerful in battle and routed foreign armies. Women received back their dead, raised to life again. Others were tortured and refused to be released, so that they might gain a better resurrection. Some faced jeers and flogging, while still others were chained and put in prison. They were stoned; they were sawed in two; they were put to death by the sword. They went about in sheepskins and goatskins, destitute, persecuted and mistreated—the world was not worthy of them. They wandered in deserts and mountains, and in caves and holes in the ground. These were all commended for their faith, yet none of them received what had been promised. God had planned something better for us so that only together with us would they be made perfect.

UNDERSTANDING:

1. According to this chapter, were the saints of old looking forward to the promised land of Canaan or to the promise of the new earth?
2. What did they consider themselves on this present earth?

WISDOM:

Which is the real world—the one we experience with all of our senses, or the invisible world that we know by faith? For which world should we be training our children?

NOTES

_____

_____

_____

_____

_____

_____

_____

_____

_____

_____

_____

_____

_____

_____

Chapter 9

Alternatives

All your sons will be taught by the LORD, and great will be your children's peace.

—Isaiah 54:13

BEFORE PRESENTING CHRISTIAN alternatives to State education, I want to address two lies that are prevalent among Christians concerning education. The first is that going to a State school will make a student stronger in the faith, because he always has to defend it. The second is that children who attend Christian schools or home schools are not prepared to face the world. Many Christians justify sending their children to State schools on these grounds.

First of all, the fact that a student constantly has to defend his faith is proof that he is in enemy territory. One would not constantly be on the defensive if he were not constantly under attack. There is not one instance in Scripture where God encourages Christians to get their training in the enemy camp. He never says, "Learn the ways of the world, so you can be a better Christian." Nobody trains their troops for battle in the enemy's boot camp. When children attend a State school, they are not trained to contend with the world, they are trained to conform to the world.

Secondly, where is the evidence that kids who attend Christian schools are not prepared to face the world? The examples of David, Solomon, and Daniel strongly refute that argument. They were all trained by God and they were all international figures. One may argue that Christian school graduates look and feel out of place in the world, but that is because they have been trained all their lives to confront the culture, not to conform to it. That is the whole point of Christian education. We should all be uncomfortable in the world. It is the people who are comfortable in the world who can't face the world. You can't face something you are part of. This is why we need to find alternatives to State education.

We have seen from the examples of David and Daniel that God is an expert teacher. Can we still entrust our children's education to him today in our advanced techno-world? Paul gives us this answer in Colossians: "My purpose is that they may be encouraged in heart and united in love, so that they may have the full riches of *complete understanding,* in order that they may know the mystery of God, namely, *Christ, in whom are hidden all the treasures of wisdom and knowledge"* (Colossians 2:2-3). There is no knowledge apart from Christ. There is no wisdom apart from Christ. A few lines down, Paul continues, "See to it that no one takes you captive through hollow and deceptive philosophy, which depends on human tradition and the basic principles of this world rather than on Christ" (Colossians 2:8). If we give our children an education apart from Christ, we cheat them out of their rightful inheritance.

When God first commanded the Israelites to teach their children all the things he had commanded them, he did not limit the scope of education to religious teaching. Israelites had to teach their children to read, to do math, to understand science, to memorize history, to study social relationships, civics, agriculture, husbandry, medicine, and law. They had to teach the children all of these things so they would have an understanding of dietary and hygiene regulations, treatment of illness, disease, mold and mildew, law enforcement, management of animals and property, business administration, and an understanding of their roles and responsibilities in personal relationships. These instructions were in addition to religious requirements. History was of utmost importance—it had to be memorized—because it is His Story. When God said to teach these things to your children, he was talking about all of education.

Paul reinforced this idea when he wrote that fathers are responsible for the education of their children. God commands us to promulgate a biblical worldview by passing it down from parents to children. The transmission of knowledge must always be done within the context of unconditional love. It is not to be done under the threat of the sword. The only certification we need is the certification we get from God. God gives every parent the credentials to teach. Therefore, we need to seriously consider the alternatives to State schools.

The most obvious alternative for those who have children already in school would be a transfer to a Christian school. The biggest hurdles to this would be the tuition and distance from your home. The other option is homeschooling, which would require that one parent stay at home with the children and become their teacher. These may seem like insurmountable obstacles that require a great deal of sacrifice, but that will be addressed in the next chapter. For now, we will focus on the advantages of Christian education and what to look for in Christian schools.

Not all Christian schools teach a biblical worldview. Many Christian schools use the same textbooks as the State schools but throw in a Bible or religion class. These schools do not rate significantly higher in graduating students with a biblical worldview. Look for a Christian worldview school that uses textbooks written from a biblical perspective. The focus of each class should be honoring Christ, "taking every thought captive to Christ."

Christian worldview schools typically do not hire teachers who have been State certified. Instead they hire teachers from Christian colleges and universities or Bible colleges. This is done to ensure that the teacher has a biblical worldview and has been trained in teaching methods that are consistent with sound biblical principles. Teachers are expected to attend continuing education seminars and be active in their churches. They are encouraged to pray for each individual student every day and in some cases to keep written journals.

Make sure the school is a parent-run school. Most Christian schools are. This follows the biblical mandate that parents be in charge of their children's education. Parents make up the school board and decide on the curriculum. Parents often work at the school on a volunteer basis to decrease the cost of tuition. They take on anything from office work to custodial work. Not only is their presence at the school emotionally and psychologically beneficial to the students, but many parents receive free tuition for their children in exchange for taking a volunteer job at the school.

A good Christian school should offer apologetics classes to juniors and seniors, which specifically train students to defend the biblical worldview against the prevailing cultural philosophies of the day. These classes are invaluable for those students who will later attend a secular university. (University professors are trained to devour incoming Christian freshmen for lunch, but freshmen who are well-trained will not take the bait. It may save their souls.) These classes will be beneficial no matter where they go in life, because Christians are always called upon to give an answer for their faith to an unbelieving world. Many of these classes also include brief studies of other religions, which helps students recognize the uniqueness of Christianity and how to defend it when they are with people of other faiths.

Do not expect the students at Christian schools to be perfect. They get into trouble and rebel just like the rest of us. But there is comfort in knowing that the parents of your children's peers share your values. In many schools, parents are screened before they can enroll their children in the school. They must sign a written profession of faith and show that they are active in their churches. When parents, teachers, and staff are all of one accord, they can reinforce what you are teaching your children at home.

Students graduating from Christian schools typically score significantly higher on SAT and ACT tests. Many Christian schools boast a

100% college acceptance rate of graduating seniors. This also shows that the literacy rate at these schools is 100%.

The greatest advantage of a Christian school over the State school is the fact that the child is given every possible spiritual protection. He not only has the prayers of his parents, but of his teachers as well. He is indoctrinated in the Scriptures, memorizing Scripture passages every week. Paul says, "Finally, be strong in the Lord and in his mighty power. Put on the full armor of God so that you can take your stand against the devil's schemes. For our struggle is not against flesh and blood, but against the rulers, against the authorities, against the powers of this dark world and against the spiritual forces of evil in the heavenly realms" (Ephesians 6:10-12). Satan has a tough time targeting children who are protected by the armor of prayer. He has a tougher time when he can't rely on their peers to bring them down.

While all these advantages are good, parents are still responsible for educating their children in the faith. The school is there to support what you are doing at home, not to supplant it. You must remain vigilant and aware of what is taught in every class.

For many families, Christian schools may not be an option. Not every locale has a Christian school, or the cost may be prohibitive. A second option, and perhaps a better and more ideal option, is homeschooling. If you feel totally inadequate to do this job, welcome to the family. Those who feel adequate are a very small minority. Many parents who are now successfully homeschooling their children once believed they could never do it. They believed their cildren would never listen to them, or they were not organized enough, or they were not knowledgeable enough—the list goes on. There are parents out there who do not even have a high school diploma who, in obedience to God, are homeschooling their children. God is faithful: the mean performance of homeschooled students whose parents *do not have a high school diploma* is much higher than the public school national average![46] For the last ten years in a row homeschooled students have taken the highest scores nationally on the ACT test, and this past year (2008), a group of homeschooled students won the World

Championship in Robotics. Homeschooled students who had a parent with teacher certification had no advantage over those who did not. God works through our weakness.

The most obvious advantage to homeschooling is that you can give your child all the advantages of a private Christian education for under $500 a year—less than a TV set. If you buy used books, it is considerably less than that. Homeschooling is affordable for even the poorest. Many of our forefathers were not materially rich, but they were schooled at home and had a better education than they could get in any State school today.

This will come as a surprise, but one of the primary reasons Christians homeschool their children is the socialization factor. Our culture perpetuates the lie that children need to be with children their own age in order to be socialized. This pernicious lie has destroyed many children. When children as young as five to seven years of age are removed from their homes for the better part of the day, and further separated from their siblings by age-graded classrooms, the emotional effect can be devastating. At this age, children still need the comfort of knowing Mommy is close by. They still need to reach out and touch you on occasion, if only for a moment. They need to be in an environment where they are surrounded by the unconditional love and support of family members.

When children are forced to go to school at this young age, they are not in an environment of unconditional love, but in an environment of competition. They not only have to compete for the teacher's attention, but they have to compete for acceptance by their peers. Overt hostility is no stranger to the classroom. Children can be cruel, and it isn't just the school bully who is to blame. Even nice children can be cruel, and at school it is socially acceptable to tease children who are different. A child who cries for her mommy at school will be ridiculed and humiliated, and she learns quickly to stop "being a baby." The fact of the matter is, she still needs her mommy, but in the absence of parents or siblings she will ultimately bond with her peers.

These peer relationships are critical because peer bonding leads to peer dependency, and peer dependency results in conformity to the peer group. Parents are often amazed when their ten-to-twelve year-old children no longer respect them, but instead rely on their peers for counsel. In order for a child to be accepted by his peer group, he has to conform. (This is why early-age compulsory education plays so nicely into the State's agenda of consensus and conformity.) Nonconformity leads to rejection by the only real family a child has at school—the ones who were there for him when he felt abandoned at the school yard at the age of five. The child who becomes peer dependent will build a lifelong habit of insecurity, because peers will never give him unconditional love.

Research has shown that children who start school between the ages of eight and ten do better in all areas than children who start school at younger ages. The Hewitt Research Foundation published *School Can Wait,* which documents ten years worth of research on early child development and includes results of 7,000 studies that included 3,500 schools and 80,000 children. The specialists involved in the research included experts in the fields of attachment, cognition, learning, neurophysiology, parenting, perception, psychiatry, public policy, reading, and vision. Here are some of their conclusions:

- **Moore and Moore recommended ages eight to ten for beginning formal school** instruction. They suggest normally starting the child with his chronological peers—that is, starting an eight year old in the second or third grade. They point out that most late starters, usually without formal training before their first school enrollment, quickly catch up academically and often pass their more school-experienced peers. **And the late starters generally excel in behavior, sociality, and leadership...in the long run such late starters bring more joy than trouble to the classroom.**[47]
- Most people still accept the family as the primary educational delivery system for young children. **In fact, even while the trend moves**

toward earlier schooling, psychologists are pointing more and more to the home. ...Schools may be able to provide surrogate care and training for young children whose homes are inadequate...**but schools are still institutionalized,** and most of their programs tend to be structured. Research definitely questions the profitability of structured programs for most young children.[48]

- A large body of research confirms the necessity of continuous early education for young children, but the *kind* of education is the question. Research also confirms the fact that parents are the most influential educators of their own children. What parents do in a child's early years in managing the environment, being models for the child, and giving information influences both directly and indirectly a child's intellectual performance during these years and later on in school. **And the value of a strong attachment, undiluted by out-of-home care, is far more urgent for efficient and effective learning—including later school—than commonly understood.**[49]

- From findings such as these, **Schaefer concluded that the education profession can best serve children by training and educating parents to care for and educate their own children.** This supports Burton White's thesis that parent education should receive top priority in education planning, together with Gordon's suggestion that parenthood education is an effective means for bringing about social change.[50]

Imagine that! Research confirms that God's way is the best way. The one thing that researchers found over and over again is that the child's formative years last much longer than typically believed—up to eight to ten years.

Children who are schooled at home during these critical years are not nearly as susceptible to peer dependency. Homeschooled children are characterized by deep family loyalty. Unconditional love at home gives them a sense of security and confidence that schooled children rarely have. In addition, children who spend their days with parents and siblings are in a natural environment with respect to varying ages. Older siblings help the younger ones, and younger ones respect the older ones. They are taught the value of self-denial and self-sacrifice for the good of the family, rather than the value of self-actualization. They learn to question everything and think independently rather than striving for consensus.

Schools, on the other hand, provide unrealistic and overwhelmingly negative socialization. Segregating children by age is a damaging artificial construct because they will never be in a real-life situation like that again. When they join the workforce, they will be with people of all ages. It is also damaging because not all children of the same age advance at the same rate. Some may excel in reading and be slow in math. It doesn't matter—they stay at the same grade level.

Homeschoolers are all over the board because they can advance in a given subject as soon as they pass the requirements. It is not at all unusual for a seven-year-old homeschooler to be doing second-grade math and sixth-grade reading. This is much more in line with what the Bible says about training a child in the way *he* should go—following his bent and individualizing his instruction.

Homeschoolers have no lack of outside socialization. They have friends at church, on sports teams, in drama and debate classes, in their neighborhoods, within their homeschool co-ops—they actually end up having a broader range of friends than kids who grow up with the same set of friends in school. Homeschooled students average 5.2 outside activities and watch less than half as much TV as students who attend school.

Many homeschoolers have immaculate homes in spite of having children at home all day long. Household duties are part of the children's training. Children do their assigned chores, which may include dusting, vacuuming, and scouring bathrooms for the younger children, and laundry, cooking, and baking for older students. When classes are finished, usually around mid-day, many families have everyone go to their own rooms for an hour or two of quiet time. The youngest children may nap while the older ones do homework. This gives mom a much needed break to either catch up on other things or take a nap herself. (If you decide to take up homeschooling, this afternoon siesta is highly recommended!)

Parents who have removed their children from State schools in order to homeschool have said they initially worried about several things: 1) My kids will miss their friends, 2) My kids will not mind me, 3) My kids fight with each other. These are valid concerns, but they should never be the reason to leave children in the State school. What these parents are now discovering is that these problems gradually disappear. Children still play with their old friends after school, but they also make a lot of new friends in their new activities. Unexpected benefits include the fact that children have a new-found respect for their parents. When parents spend several hours of one-on-one time with a child every week, that child feels unconditional love. She thrives on the attention and she begins to see her parents as the ones to go to for answers to questions. Respect for parents is a natural result of homeschooling.

Sibling rivalry decreases dramatically because competition for attention is no longer necessary. Younger children love it when older children help them with their schoolwork, and the older children feel needed and important when they help the younger ones. Homeschooling can right many dysfunctions.

Since schoolwork takes only a few hours a day for the elementary grades, there is plenty of time to do fun things as a family. It is a reward for hard work. Homeschooled children can spend their afternoons at a park or a museum, and many homeschool families take advantage of traveling off-season. High school students often complete between fifteen and thirty hours of college credit courses by the time they graduate high school, which gives them a decided advantage over their peers.

As adults, homeschooled students are more likely to own their own businesses and work from home. They engage their children in the business and make it a family endeavor. They are less focused on climbing the corporate ladder and more focused on family.

Christian schools and home schools are both biblically-based options for covenant children. Another consideration when looking at alternatives for education is whether to stay with traditional curricula or go classical. Classical education is based on the Trivium—a three-part curriculum that is based on the developmental stages of learning. In the first stage, the grammar stage, which is roughly grades one through four, children love to memorize and are capable of memorizing long passages of Scripture or multiplication tables. They may not have a complete understanding of what they are memorizing, but that doesn't really matter at this point. The important thing is to get the facts down. This stage corresponds to what the Bible refers to as getting knowledge.

In the second stage, the logic stage, generally grades five through eight, children begin to think for themselves, and they love to argue. In every class the focus is on thinking logically (as opposed to the anti-logic of the Hegelian dialectic). They are taught to analyze arguments, identify logical fallacies, and build logical arguments of their own. This stage corresponds to what the Bible calls understanding. It includes the ability to derive principles from the stated facts.

The third stage, the rhetoric stage, typically the high school years, makes use of the students' needs to express themselves. These years focus on speech, debate, oratory, forensics, and writing. It corresponds to biblical wisdom, being able to apply principles to daily life. Each stage builds on the one before it.

In all three stages, reading and writing are of paramount importance. Reading is from the great books rather than contemporary textbooks. A student will study original documents and biographies rather than a modern-day summary. He will read *Mein Kampf* rather than read a textbook analysis of Hitler. World history from creation to the present is studied in four-year segments and repeated three times between grades one and twelve. Children are taught Latin in grade school. Although some consider Latin to be a dead language, it is the key to all the Romance languages. A thorough knowledge of Latin will enable a student to virtually read the romance languages (Spanish, French, Portuguese,

Romanian, and Italian) without ever having studied them, because ninety percent of their roots are derived from Latin. Also, anyone who wants to enter the fields of medicine, science, or law will greatly benefit from Latin. Latin considerably increases a student's vocabulary.

Many new Christian Classical schools are starting up every year because of increased demand. Many of these Christian schools are university-model schools, which means students can sign up and pay for only those courses they need. These schools are homeschool-friendly and parents can take advantage of signing up for classes they feel uncomfortable teaching themselves. Classical education was the norm when this country was founded, and we need only read the works of our founding fathers to be impressed with the degree of education they had. Statesmen and orators flourished during that time and the literacy rate was ninety-nine percent.

It is interesting that the classical methods of teaching correspond to what the Bible teaches in regard to methodology. It is the way teachers have taught for millennia. It works because it was designed by God. Acquire knowledge, apply understanding, and impart wisdom. Traditional methods used in the State schools no longer stress memorization because they say the children don't understand what they are learning anyway. Why memorize the multiplication tables when you can use a calculator? They apply anti-logic in the form of the Hegelian dialectic, and they impart foolishness.

The alternatives to State education are available to everyone. It doesn't matter how rich or poor you are. It doesn't matter if there is a Christian school in your neighborhood or not. We may have obstacles in meeting God's requirements for the education of our children, but there is really no excuse we can give for failing to follow God's instructions in this matter.

Soli Deo Gloria

FURTHER UP
AND
FURTHER IN

WEEK NINE—DAY ONE

A Study in Proverbs

KNOWLEDGE:

Proverbs 1

Prologue: Purpose and Theme
1 The proverbs of Solomon son of David, king of Israel:
2 for attaining wisdom and discipline;
  for understanding words of insight;
3 for acquiring a disciplined and prudent life,
  doing what is right and just and fair;
4 for giving prudence to the simple,
  knowledge and discretion to the young—
5 let the wise listen and add to their learning,
  and let the discerning get guidance—
6 for understanding proverbs and parables,
  the sayings and riddles of the wise.
7 The fear of the LORD is the beginning of knowledge,
  but fools despise wisdom and discipline.

Exhortations to Embrace Wisdom
Warning against Enticement

8 Listen, my son, to your father's instruction
  and do not forsake your mother's teaching.
  and a chain to adorn your neck.
10 My son, if sinners entice you,
  do not give in to them.
11 If they say, "Come along with us;
  let's lie in wait for someone's blood,
  let's waylay some harmless soul;

12 let's swallow them alive, like the grave
  and whole, like those who go down to the pit;
13 we will get all sorts of valuable things
  and fill our houses with plunder;
14 throw in your lot with us,
  and we will share a common purse"—
15 my son, do not go along with them,
  do not set foot on their paths;
16 for their feet rush into sin,
  they are swift to shed blood.
17 How useless to spread a net
  in full view of all the birds!
18 These men lie in wait for their own blood;
  they waylay only themselves!
19 Such is the end of all who go after ill-gotten gain;
  it takes away the lives of those who get it.

Warning against Rejecting Wisdom

20 Wisdom calls aloud in the street,
  she raises her voice in the public squares;
21 at the head of the noisy streets she cries out,
  in the gateways of the city she makes her speech:
22 "How long will you simple ones love your simple ways?
  How long will mockers delight in mockery
  and fools hate knowledge?
23 If you had responded to my rebuke,
  I would have poured out my heart to you
  and made my thoughts known to you.
24 But since you rejected me when I called
  and no one gave heed when I stretched out my hand,
25 since you ignored all my advice
  and would not accept my rebuke,

26 I in turn will laugh at your disaster;
  I will mock when calamity overtakes you—
27 when calamity overtakes you like a storm,
  when disaster sweeps over you like a whirlwind,
  when distress and trouble overwhelm you.
28 "Then they will call to me but I will not answer;
  they will look for me but will not find me.
29 Since they hated knowledge
  and did not choose to fear the LORD,
30 since they would not accept my advice
  and spurned my rebuke,
31 they will eat the fruit of their ways
  and be filled with the fruit of their schemes.
32 For the waywardness of the simple will kill them,
  and the complacency of fools will destroy them;
33 but whoever listens to me will live in safety
  and be at ease, without fear of harm."

UNDERSTANDING AND WISDOM:

1. What is the purpose of the Proverbs?
2. Who are assumed to be the teachers of children?
3. In verses 29-31, how is hating true knowledge again compared to eating the fruit of the forbidden tree? Is the consequence the same?
4. How are knowledge, understanding, and wisdom related to discipline and living a prudent life?

NOTES

Week Nine—Day Two

A Study in Proverbs

KNOWLEDGE:

Proverbs 2

Moral Benefits of Wisdom

1 My son, if you accept my words
    and store up my commands within you,
2 turning your ear to wisdom
    and applying your heart to understanding,
3 and if you call out for insight
    and cry aloud for understanding,
    and search for it as for hidden treasure,
5 then you will understand the fear of the Lord
    and find the knowledge of God.
6 For the Lord gives wisdom,
    and from his mouth come knowledge and understanding.
7 He holds victory in store for the upright,
    he is a shield to those whose walk is blameless,
8 for he guards the course of the just
    and protects the way of his faithful ones.
9 Then you will understand what is right and just
    and fair—every good path.
10 For wisdom will enter your heart,
    and knowledge will be pleasant to your soul.
11 Discretion will protect you,
    and understanding will guard you.
12 Wisdom will save you from the ways of wicked men,
    from men whose words are perverse,
13 who leave the straight paths
    to walk in dark ways,

14 who delight in doing wrong
  and rejoice in the perverseness of evil,
15 whose paths are crooked
  and who are devious in their ways.
16 It will save you also from the adulteress,
  from the wayward wife with her seductive words,
17 who has left the partner of her youth
  and ignored the covenant she made before God.
18 For her house leads down to death
  and her paths to the spirits of the dead.
19 None who go to her return
  or attain the paths of life.
20 Thus you will walk in the ways of good men
  and keep to the paths of the righteous.
21 For the upright will live in the land,
  and the blameless will remain in it;
22 but the wicked will be cut off from the land,
  and the unfaithful will be torn from it.

UNDERSTANDING AND WISDOM:

1. If you believed there was a hidden treasure, how long and hard would you search for it?
2. How important is wisdom?
3. Where do we get God's wisdom?
4. How valuable is memorization of Scripture and an intimate familiarity with the whole Word of God?

NOTES

WEEK NINE—DAY THREE

A Study in Proverbs

KNOWLEDGE:

Proverbs 3

Further Benefits of Wisdom

1 My son, do not forget my teaching,
   but keep my commands in your heart,
2 for they will prolong your life many years
   and bring you prosperity.
3 Let love and faithfulness never leave you;
   bind them around your neck,
   write them on the tablet of your heart.
4 Then you will win favor and a good name
   in the sight of God and man.
5 Trust in the LORD with all your heart
   and lean not on your own understanding;
6 in all your ways acknowledge him,
   and he will make your paths straight.
7 Do not be wise in your own eyes;
   fear the LORD and shun evil.
8 This will bring health to your body
   and nourishment to your bones.
9 Honor the LORD with your wealth,
   with the firstfruits of all your crops;
10 then your barns will be filled to overflowing,
   and your vats will brim over with new wine.
11 My son, do not despise the LORD's discipline
   and do not resent his rebuke,
12 because the LORD disciplines those he loves,
   as a father the son he delights in.

Two Trees of Knowledge

13 Blessed is the man who finds wisdom,
  the man who gains understanding,
14 for she is more profitable than silver
  and yields better returns than gold.
15 She is more precious than rubies;
  nothing you desire can compare with her.
16 Long life is in her right hand;
  in her left hand are riches and honor.
17 Her ways are pleasant ways,
  and all her paths are peace.
18 She is a tree of life to those who embrace her;
  those who lay hold of her will be blessed.
19 By wisdom the LORD laid the earth's foundations,
  by understanding he set the heavens in place;
20 by his knowledge the deeps were divided,
  and the clouds let drop the dew.
21 My son, preserve sound judgment and discernment,
  do not let them out of your sight;
22 they will be life for you,
  an ornament to grace your neck.
23 Then you will go on your way in safety,
  and your foot will not stumble;
24 when you lie down, you will not be afraid;
  when you lie down, your sleep will be sweet.
25 Have no fear of sudden disaster
  or of the ruin that overtakes the wicked,
26 for the LORD will be your confidence
  and will keep your foot from being snared.
27 Do not withhold good from those who deserve it,
  when it is in your power to act.
28 Do not say to your neighbor,
  "Come back later; I'll give it tomorrow"—
  when you now have it with you.

29 Do not plot harm against your neighbor,
  who lives trustfully near you.
30 Do not accuse a man for no reason—
  when he has done you no harm.
31 Do not envy a violent man
  or choose any of his ways,
32 for the LORD detests a perverse man
  but takes the upright into his confidence.
33 The LORD's curse is on the house of the wicked,
  but he blesses the home of the righteous.
34 He mocks proud mockers
  but gives grace to the humble.
35 The wise inherit honor,
  but fools he holds up to shame.

UNDERSTANDING AND WISDOM:

1. List all the benefits of wisdom.
2. How is true wisdom once again compared to the tree of life?
3. How many times does Solomon associate wisdom with life in this chapter?

NOTES

_____

_____

_____

_____

_____

_____

_____

_____

_____

_____

_____

_____

_____

_____

_____

WEEK NINE—DAY FOUR

A Study in Proverbs

KNOWLEDGE:

PROVERBS 4

Wisdom Is Supreme

1 Listen, my sons, to a father's instruction;
  pay attention and gain understanding.
2 I give you sound learning,
  so do not forsake my teaching.
3 When I was a boy in my father's house,
  still tender, and an only child of my mother,
4 he taught me and said,
  "Lay hold of my words with all your heart;
  keep my commands and you will live.
5 Get wisdom, get understanding;
  do not forget my words or swerve from them.
6 Do not forsake wisdom, and she will protect you;
  love her, and she will watch over you.
7 Wisdom is supreme; therefore get wisdom.
  Though it cost all you have, get understanding.
8 Esteem her, and she will exalt you;
  embrace her, and she will honor you.
9 She will set a garland of grace on your head
  and present you with a crown of splendor."
10 Listen, my son, accept what I say,
  and the years of your life will be many.
11 I guide you in the way of wisdom
  and lead you along straight paths.
12 When you walk, your steps will not be hampered;
  when you run, you will not stumble.

13 Hold on to instruction, do not let it go;
  guard it well, for it is your life.
14 Do not set foot on the path of the wicked
  or walk in the way of evil men.
15 Avoid it, do not travel on it;
  turn from it and go on your way.
16 For they cannot sleep till they do evil;
  they are robbed of slumber till they make someone fall.
17 They eat the bread of wickedness
  and drink the wine of violence.
18 The path of the righteous is like the first gleam of dawn,
  shining ever brighter till the full light of day.
19 But the way of the wicked is like deep darkness;
  they do not know what makes them stumble.
20 My son, pay attention to what I say;
  listen closely to my words.
21 Do not let them out of your sight,
  keep them within your heart;
22 for they are life to those who find them
  and health to a man's whole body.
23 Above all else, guard your heart,
  for it is the wellspring of life.
24 Put away perversity from your mouth;
  keep corrupt talk far from your lips.
25 Let your eyes look straight ahead,
  fix your gaze directly before you.
26 Make level paths for your feet
  and take only ways that are firm.
27 Do not swerve to the right or the left;
  keep your foot from evil.

UNDERSTANDING AND WISDOM:

1. List all the things Solomon advises his sons to do in regard to wisdom.
2. What does he warn against?
3. What are we to guard above all else?

NOTES

_____

_____

_____

_____

_____

_____

_____

_____

_____

_____

_____

_____

_____

_____

_____

_____

WEEK NINE—DAY FIVE

A Study in Proverbs

KNOWLEDGE:

Proverbs 9

Invitations of Wisdom and of Folly
1 Wisdom has built her house;
  she has hewn out its seven pillars.
2 She has prepared her meat and mixed her wine;
  she has also set her table.
3 She has sent out her maids, and she calls
  from the highest point of the city.
4 "Let all who are simple come in here!"
  she says to those who lack judgment.
5 "Come, eat my food
  and drink the wine I have mixed.
6 Leave your simple ways and you will live;
  walk in the way of understanding.
7 "Whoever corrects a mocker invites insult;
  whoever rebukes a wicked man incurs abuse.
8 Do not rebuke a mocker or he will hate you;
  rebuke a wise man and he will love you.
9 Instruct a wise man and he will be wiser still;
  teach a righteous man and he will add to his learning.
10 "The fear of the LORD is the beginning of wisdom,
  and knowledge of the Holy One is understanding.
11 For through me your days will be many,
  and years will be added to your life.
12 If you are wise, your wisdom will reward you;
  if you are a mocker, you alone will suffer."
13 The woman Folly is loud;

she is undisciplined and without knowledge.
14 She sits at the door of her house,
  on a seat at the highest point of the city,
15 calling out to those who pass by,
  who go straight on their way.
16 "Let all who are simple come in here!"
  she says to those who lack judgment.
17 "Stolen water is sweet;
  food eaten in secret is delicious!"
18 But little do they know that the dead are there,
  that her guests are in the depths of the grave.

UNDERSTANDING AND WISDOM:

1. How do Wisdom and Folly represent the two trees of knowledge?
2. To whom do they each call out?
3. Do you sense a competition here? Who are the trophies in this competition?
4. Who are the trophies in the cosmic battle today?
5. What are the consequences for those who partake of the meat and wine of Wisdom?
6. What are the consequences for those who partake of the stolen water and food that must be eaten in secret?

NOTES

_____

_____

_____

_____

_____

_____

_____

_____

_____

_____

_____

_____

_____

_____

_____

_____

Chapter 10

The Cost of Discipleship

Wisdom is supreme; therefore get wisdom. Though it cost all you have, get understanding.

—Proverbs 4:7

IN CHAPTER ONE, we examined the way Jesus defined eternal life: "that they may know you, the only true God, and Jesus Christ whom you have sent" (John 17:3). This kind of knowing is a deep, intimate relationship that only comes through hard work. If you are married, you have an idea how much work it takes to maintain the relationship. It is hard work to know God and to know Christ, but the knowing is eternal life. Paul says,

What is more, I consider everything a loss compared to the surpassing greatness of knowing Christ Jesus my Lord, for whose sake I have lost all things. I consider them rubbish, that I may gain Christ and be found in him, not having a righteousness of my own that comes from the law but that which is through faith in Christ—the righteousness that comes from God and is by faith. I want to know Christ and the power of his resurrection and the fellowship of sharing his sufferings, becoming like him in his death.

—Philippians 3:8-10

Paul considers everything a loss compared to knowing Christ! He wants to share in Christ's sufferings, even if it means death. This is not a new idea. It has been God's desire from the beginning of time that we would want to know him. He says, "For I delight in loyalty rather than sacrifice, and in the knowledge of God rather than burnt offerings" (Hosea 6:6). To Jeremiah, he says, "Thus says the LORD, 'Let not the wise man boast in his wisdom, let not the mighty man boast in his might, let not the rich man boast in his riches, but let him who boasts boast in this, that he understands and knows me'" (Jeremiah 9:23-24 ESV). We must be willing to give up everything in order to have this knowledge. We must be willing to suffer great loss.

Our culture teaches us from kindergarten up that the goal of our lives should be self-actualization. Self-actualization is the pinnacle of Maslow's hierarchy of needs. We are driven to dream big, to follow our inner desires, to be everything we can be. We believe this lie and then try to bring God into it by convincing ourselves that we are just trying to be all that God wants us to be. Isn't that how fathers justify abandoning their families to climb the corporate ladder? Isn't that how mothers justify a career that takes them away from their babies? We tell ourselves it's for the family. We need the money to buy a house or a car or whatever. Rubbish. We think we are sacrificing ourselves for our children, when we are really sacrificing our children to satisfy ourselves.

Jesus understood the cost of knowing God. He spent his entire earthly life showing us what that involved. It involves suffering. It involves total submission to the will of the Father. It involves death to self. Shortly after Jesus told his disciples about his own impending death, he said these words, "If anyone would come after me, he must deny himself, take up his cross and follow me. For whoever wants to save his life will lose it, but whoever loses his life for me will find it. What good will it be for a man if he gains the whole world, yet forfeits his soul? Or what can a man give in exchange for his soul?" (Matthew 16:24-26). The cost of discipleship is our lives. Christ expects us to lay down our lives, to deny ourselves all the things we think we have coming to us, to sacrifice everything in order to be his followers.

As parents, the highest goal we should have for our children should be that they know God in a deep and intimate way that brings eternal life. We should be willing to lay down everything in our lives that interferes with that goal. A Christian education is what God demands for his covenant children. To do anything less, to turn God's children over to the State for their education is a violation of biblical principles as well as a violation of the vows we made when our children were dedicated or baptized.

We are fortunate in this country to have alternatives to State education, but both alternatives are costly—either costly financially or costly in terms of time, effort, and convenience. Mothers may have to give up a career to homeschool. That is costly. Families may have to sacrifice their current standard of living. A complete change of lifestyle may be necessary. But consider this: we still have alternatives. In Germany that is no longer the case. In Germany, homeschooling has been outlawed on the grounds of "worldview incompatibility." Homeschoolers typically do not share the worldview of the State, whose goals are to produce citizens who will benefit the global economy. Parents have been imprisoned and had their children taken as wards of the State for the simple crime of homeschooling.[51] Some families have already fled the country to avoid prosecution. Homeschooling in America is not nearly as costly as homeschooling in Germany, but every day the U.S. courts are trying to find ways to put an end to our alternatives.

Jesus understood the conflicts we would have with the State, and what it would cost us to be faithful. John Piper, author of *What Jesus Demands of the World,* comments on this cost:

> Jesus warns of impending conflict. He tells his disciples they will have to choose between allegiance to him and allegiance to Caesar's State. This will cost some of them their lives. "They will lay their hands

on you and persecute you, delivering you up to the synagogues and prisons, and you will be brought before kings and governors for my name's sake...some of you they will put to death" (Luke 21:12,16). The only way this warning makes sense is if Jesus is telling us not to render to Caesar everything that Caesar thinks is Caesar's. Rendering to Caesar the things that are Caesar's does not include rendering obedience to Caesar's demand that we not render supreme allegiance to God. God's supreme authority limits the authority of Caesar and the allegiance we owe him.[52]

In our country, the National Education Association has recommended that homeschooling be outlawed. So far, God has prevented that from happening.

Many parents believe that the alternatives to State education are just impossible for their families. The schools are too far away or too expensive. Homeschooling is out of the question because their children do not listen to them or because mom is not cut out for the job. Mom needs a break from the kids. Both parents work to make ends meet and barely pay the bills. What would happen if they added thousands of dollars for tuition to their budget? How would they pay the bills if mom quit her job to homeschool?

These are all valid concerns, but consider a few things. First of all, we will not get anywhere if we are looking to ourselves to overcome insurmountable obstacles. God never asks us to do something without equipping us to do it. We may not always know how he will do it, but we must have faith that he will. Secondly, nothing is impossible for God. He loves making miraculous provisions for us. Our problem is that we like to play it safe and never give him the opportunity. It takes faith to move mountains. Obedience comes first and miracles follow. Finally, we need to examine ourselves to evaluate whether or not the obstacles are really insurmountable. Maybe the truth is that they are only insurmountable if we don't change anything else. Sending our kids to Christian schools may require a drastic change in lifestyle. It may require downsizing, getting a smaller house, or selling a car. The truth may be that we ourselves are the biggest obstacle. The truth may be that we fear losing all those things we want to hang on to.

Fear of insurmountable obstacles has always kept God's people from experiencing his miracles and his blessings. Numbers chapter 13 tells a story about twelve spies who went out to explore the land of Canaan. The Israelites had been traveling to the land God had promised to Abraham centuries before. They were finally ready to enter the land. The twelve spies explored the Promised Land for forty days. They reported that the land was rich, flowing with milk and honey. They brought back some of its fruit to prove their point. But ten of the spies were convinced it would be impossible for the Israelites to take the land. They said, "The people who live there are powerful, and the cities are fortified and very large." They spread fear among the people. Only two spies, Caleb and Joshua, said, "We should go up and take possession of the land, for we can certainly do it." This made the ten spies look like cowards, so they spread lies about the land saying, "The land we explored devours those living in it. All the people we saw there are of great size. We saw the Nephilim there…We seemed like grasshoppers in our own eyes, and we looked the same to them."

That night the Israelites bemoaned their fate. They slandered God and said he only brought them out of Egypt to kill them with a sword. They decided to elect a leader who would bring them back into captivity in Egypt. They would rather live in captivity than risk obedience to God and experience his rich blessings. They wanted to play it safe and depend on themselves. These are the very same people who had just witnessed the power of the ten plagues against Egypt! These are the very people who walked across the sea on dry ground! What were they thinking? Their response angered Joshua and Caleb, who tore their garments and said to the entire assembly, "The land we passed through and explored is exceedingly good. If the LORD is pleased with us, he will lead us into that land, a land flowing with milk and honey, and will give it to us.

Only do not rebel against the LORD. And do not be afraid of the people in the land, because we will swallow them up. Their protection is gone, but the LORD is with us. Do not be afraid of them."

The people became so angry at this that they threatened to stone their leaders. At this point, God intervened and told Moses he would destroy them and make a new nation from him. Moses pleaded with God to spare them, and God did. But he made them wander in the wilderness for forty years, one year for every day of exploration by the spies. Only when everyone who was twenty years old or over had died, would they enter the land. Joshua and Caleb were the exceptions.

Do you feel afraid to step out in faith? We all do at times when God forces us to let go of the things we depend on. Talk to people who homeschool their children or send them to Christian schools. Ask them how they do it. You may be surprised to see that a majority of them have a story to tell about God's miraculous provision for their families and how he has enriched their lives with his blessings. My own father was an "eggman" in the 1950's. He went door-to-door selling eggs and poultry to his customers. My mother stayed at home with five kids. I will never know how they did it, but they managed to put five kids through one of the best Christian schools in the country. Today the tuition for one child is more than my dad made in a year. We very rarely went out to eat. My mother made our clothes. We could rarely afford a family vacation. For entertainment, we would visit friends or invite them over.

I did not have many of the things some of my friends at school had—large homes, swimming pools, and clothes from Marshall Fields. I guess we were poor, but I never knew it. We always had food on the table and warmth in winter. I felt secure as a child. It never occurred to me that I might be missing something. I never suffered from peer dependency because my family was my support group. We had family devotions twice a day, at breakfast and dinner. My parents would pray with me at night before I went to bed. God was there. What was there to be afraid of? My teachers at school taught us the same stories I heard from my dad at home. We sang the same songs in school that we sang in Sunday school. It was a consistent, integrated life.

Did I appreciate it? No, I took it for granted. I never thought about thanking my parents for their incredible sacrifice. In fact, it got worse. There was a time after I left home when I felt the whole thing was a sham. I feared I had been brainwashed and I felt God had abandoned me. I stopped attending church and started on my own little detour. No doubt my parents thought all their hard work and sacrifice went right down the drain. But somewhere deep within, I knew the truth. Inside my mind, inside my heart was the roadmap that brought me home. I have my parents and my teachers to thank for that. Had it not been for a thoroughly integrated Christian education, I might have been one of the casualties in the cosmic battle. Had there been teachers in my past who taught me there was no God, I may have stayed away for good. But God was faithful to my parents. It was *their* obedience he honored.

Take another look at this verse from Hosea: "My people are destroyed from lack of knowledge. Because you have rejected knowledge, I also reject you as my priests; because you have ignored the law of your God, I also will ignore your children" (Hosea 4:6). These were dark days in the history of Israel. To all appearances, Satan was winning the cosmic battle. Isaiah prophesied that Israel would be taken captive by her enemies. Although a remnant of the people was faithful to God, they too would be taken captive. This is what God promised them:

> Those who hope in me will not be disappointed. Can plunder be taken from warriors or captives rescued from the fierce? But this is what the LORD says, "Yes, captives will be taken from warriors, and plunder retrieved from the fierce. I will contend with those who contend with you, and your children I will save…Then all mankind will know that I the LORD, am your Savior, your Redeemer, the Mighty One of Jacob."
>
> —Isaiah 49:23-26

Christians can be taken captive. Maybe your son or daughter will be one of them. The promise here is to *save your children,* and the promise is to *those who put their hope in God.* He does not give this promise to those who reject his precepts. Just the opposite—he says "I also will ignore your children." My parents put their hope in him. They obeyed him by giving me the fruit of the tree of (eternal) life and by keeping me far from the fruit of the tree of the knowledge of good and evil, which would have poisoned my soul. They laid down their lives for me.

Imagine what it must have been like to be Mary and Joseph. God entrusted them with the training of his own son. This son would one day have to fight all the demons of hell. How does one prepare a child for that? Jesus had to be prepared to face the temptations in the desert, to perform miracles, to completely submit to the Father, to face humiliation, torture, and death. If you were responsible for his upbringing, would you not sacrifice everything to give him the godliest training available? How would it feel to know that your very salvation depended on his success? Christian parents, your children are from God. He gave them to you because he desires godly offspring. You do not know your child's future. You have no idea what demons or persecutions he may face in this life. You don't know if or when or how your child may be taken captive. Are you arming him for the battle? If he is taken captive, will he be able to find his way back home? Jesus said, "Whatsoever you do to the least of these, my brethren, you have done it unto me." Are you training your children the way you would have trained Jesus? It would be wrong to train them any other way.

Is it actually a sin for Christians to send their children to State schools? Many Christian leaders avoid the "s" word even when speaking out against State education. But the case has been made from Scripture that biblical principles are violated when the State takes over the education of God's covenant children. Parents further violate biblical principles by giving to Caesar what belongs to God. When we partner with the State to educate our children, we violate every prohibition given in Scripture about the deadly alliances that allow unbelievers to have authority in our lives or the lives of our children. Biblical principles are violated when we deliberately place a child in harm's way—whether physical or spiritual—and test God. When biblical principles are violated, God calls it sin. What God calls sin, we must also call sin.

Some may be thinking, "It is too late for my children. They are already in high school or college or beyond." To them I say, it is never too late. God gives his people this promise in the book of Joel, "Even now," declares the LORD, "return to me with all your heart, with fasting and weeping and mourning. Rend your heart and not your garments. Return to the LORD your God for he is gracious and compassionate, slow to anger and abounding in love, *and he relents from sending calamity"* (Joel 2:13). Unbelievable! Even now... though we think it is too late...even now he will not only forgive, but relent from sending calamity. In the same chapter, God promises to restore the years the locusts have eaten, but only if we repent. Who is guilty? We all are. The Bible says we have all sinned and come short of the glory of God. We are all in this together. Your children may be through school, but there will grandchildren and great-grandchildren. What kind of legacy will you leave them? As long as you are alive, you can still lay down your lives for them.

God intended for us to be people who lay down our lives—our careers, our interests, our dreams, our pursuit of happiness—for others. It is the cost of discipleship. Jesus said, "Greater love has no one than this, that one lay down his life for his friends" (John 15:13). Remember though, that when you lay down your life, it isn't forever. Jesus promises that anyone who loses his life will find it. We have all of eternity to do whatever we want to do, and be all that we ever hope to be. We have the promise of heaven waiting for us.

The writer of Hebrews says we have a great cloud of witnesses cheering us on—all those who have gone before us. My parents are in that cloud of witnesses. They have left me with a legacy that I want to pass on to my children and grandchildren and to all who will follow until that great and glorious appearing of our Lord and Savior, Jesus Christ. It is my prayer that others will do the same. *Soli Deo Gloria.*

Soli Deo Gloria

FURTHER UP
AND
FURTHER IN

WEEK TEN—DAY ONE

Though It Cost All You Have

KNOWLEDGE:

John 17:3

Now this is eternal life: that they may know you, the only true God, and Jesus Christ, whom you have sent.

1 Corinthians 1:22-24

Jews demand miraculous signs and Greeks look for wisdom, but we preach Christ crucified: a stumbling block to Jews and foolishness to Gentiles, but to those whom God has called, both Jews and Greeks, Christ the power of God and the wisdom of God.

Colossians 2:2-3

My purpose is that they may be encouraged in heart and united in love, so that they may have the full riches of complete understanding, in order that they may know the mystery of God, namely, Christ, in whom are hidden all the treasures of wisdom and knowledge. Wisdom is supreme; therefore get wisdom.

Proverbs 4:7

Though it cost all you have, get understanding.

Matthew 13:44-46

The kingdom of heaven is like treasure hidden in a field. When a man found it, he hid it again, and then in his joy went and sold all he had and bought that field. Again, the kingdom of heaven is like a merchant looking for fine pearls. When he found one of great value, he went away and sold everything he had and bought it.

Matthew 16:24-27

Then Jesus said to his disciples, "If anyone would come after me, he must deny himself and take up his cross and follow me. For whoever wants to save his life will lose it, but whoever loses his life for me will find it. What good will it be for a man if he gains the whole world, yet forfeits his soul? Or what can a man give in exchange for his soul? For the Son of Man is going to come in his Father's glory with his angels, and then he will reward each person according to what he has done."

UNDERSTANDING:

1. According to John 17:3, what is eternal life?
2. According to 1 Corinthians 1:22-24 and Colossians 2:2-3, what are the attributes of Christ?
3. According to Proverbs 4:7 and Matthew 13:44-46, what should we be willing to sacrifice in order to gain this treasure?
4. What could be the consequence of not denying oneself according to Matthew 16:24-27?

WISDOM:

Does Christian education cost too much? Can we afford *not* to give our children a Christian education?

NOTES

Week Ten—Day Two

The Prophets

KNOWLEDGE:

Isaiah 20:1-6

In the year that the supreme commander, sent by Sargon king of Assyria, came to Ashdod and attacked and captured it—at that time the LORD spoke through Isaiah son of Amoz. He said to him, "Take off the sackcloth from your body and the sandals from your feet." And he did so, going around stripped and barefoot. Then the LORD said, "Just as my servant Isaiah has gone stripped and barefoot for three years, as a sign and portent against Egypt and Cush, so the king of Assyria will lead away stripped and barefoot the Egyptian captives and Cushite exiles, young and old, with buttocks bared—to Egypt's shame. Those who trusted in Cush and boasted in Egypt will be afraid and put to shame. In that day the people who live on this coast will say, 'See what has happened to those we relied on, those we fled to for help and deliverance from the king of Assyria! How then can we escape?'"

Jeremiah 10:1-9

Then the word of the LORD came to me: "You must not marry and have sons or daughters in this place." For this is what the LORD says about the sons and daughters born in this land and about the women who are their mothers and the men who are their fathers: "They will die of deadly diseases. They will not be mourned or buried but will be like refuse lying on the ground. They will perish by sword and famine, and their dead bodies will become food for the birds of the air and the beasts of the earth."

For this is what the LORD says: "Do not enter a house where there is a funeral meal; do not go to mourn or show sympathy, because I have withdrawn my blessing, my love and my pity from this people," declares the LORD. "Both high and low will die in this land. They will not be buried or mourned, and no one will cut himself or shave his head for them. No one will offer food to comfort those who mourn for the dead—not even for a father or a mother—nor will anyone give them a drink to console them.

And do not enter a house where there is feasting and sit down to eat and drink. For this is what the LORD Almighty, the God of Israel, says: "Before your eyes and in your days I will bring an end to the sounds of joy and gladness and to the voices of bride and bridegroom in this place."

Ezekiel 24:15-24

The word of the LORD came to me: "Son of man, with one blow I am about to take away from you the delight of your eyes. Yet do not lament or weep or shed any tears. Groan quietly; do not mourn for the dead. Keep your turban fastened and your sandals on your feet; do not cover the lower part of your face or eat the customary food of mourners."

So I spoke to the people in the morning, and in the evening my wife died. The next morning I did as I had been commanded. Then the people asked me, "Won't you tell us what these things have to do with us?" So I said to them, "The word of the LORD came to me: Say to the house of Israel, 'This is what the Sovereign LORD says: I am about to desecrate my sanctuary—the stronghold in which you take pride, the delight of your eyes, the object of your affection. The sons and daughters you left behind will fall by the sword. And you will do as I have done. You will not cover the lower part of your face or eat the customary food of mourners . You will keep your turbans on your heads and your sandals on your feet. You will not mourn or weep but will waste away because of your sins and groan among yourselves. Ezekiel will be a sign to you; you will do just as he has done. When this happens, you will know that I am the Sovereign LORD.'"

UNDERSTANDING:

1. List all the things Isaiah, Jeremiah, and Ezekiel were forbidden.
2. What did their obedience cost them?

WISDOM:

List the things that obedience to God in the area of education would cost you.

NOTES

WEEK TEN—DAY THREE

Paul

KNOWLEDGE:

2 Corinthians 4

Treasures in Jars of Clay

Therefore, since through God's mercy we have this ministry, we do not lose heart. Rather, we have renounced secret and shameful ways; we do not use deception, nor do we distort the word of God. On the contrary, by setting forth the truth plainly we commend ourselves to every man's conscience in the sight of God. And even if our gospel is veiled, it is veiled to those who are perishing. The god of this age has blinded the minds of unbelievers, so that they cannot see the light of the gospel of the glory of Christ, who is the image of God. For we do not preach ourselves, but Jesus Christ as Lord, and ourselves as your servants for Jesus' sake. For God, who said, "Let light shine out of darkness," made his light shine in our hearts to give us the light of the knowledge of the glory of God in the face of Christ.

But we have this treasure in jars of clay to show that this all-surpassing power is from God and not from us. We are hard pressed on every side, but not crushed; perplexed, but not in despair; persecuted, but not abandoned; struck down, but not destroyed. We always carry around in our body the death of Jesus, so that the life of Jesus may also be revealed in our body. For we who are alive are always being given over to death for Jesus' sake, so that his life may be revealed in our mortal body. So then, death is at work in us, but life is at work in you.

It is written: "I believed; therefore I have spoken." With that same spirit of faith we also believe and therefore speak, because we know that the one who raised the Lord Jesus from the dead will also raise us with Jesus and present us with you in his presence. All this is for your benefit, so that the grace that is reaching more and more people may cause thanksgiving to overflow to the glory of God.

Therefore we do not lose heart. Though outwardly we are wasting away, yet inwardly we are being renewed day by day. For our light and momentary troubles are achieving for us an eternal glory that far outweighs them all. So we fix our eyes not on what is seen, but on what is unseen. For what is seen is temporary, but what is unseen is eternal.

2 Corinthians 6:3-13

We put no stumbling block in anyone's path, so that our ministry will not be discredited. Rather, as servants of God we commend ourselves in every way: in great endurance; in troubles, hardships and distresses; in beatings, imprisonments and riots; in hard work, sleepless nights and hunger; in purity, understanding, patience and kindness; in the Holy Spirit and in sincere love; in truthful speech and in the power of God; with weapons of righteousness in the right hand and in the left; through glory and dishonor, bad report and good report; genuine, yet regarded as impostors; known, yet regarded as unknown; dying, and yet we live on; beaten, and yet not killed; sorrowful, yet always rejoicing; poor, yet making many rich; having nothing, and yet possessing everything.

We have spoken freely to you, Corinthians, and opened wide our hearts to you. We are not withholding our affection from you, but you are withholding yours from us. As a fair exchange—I speak as to my children—open wide your hearts also.

UNDERSTANDING:

1. How does Paul's life prove he is a true disciple of Christ?
2. What is the treasure he speaks of?
3. For whose benefit is Paul laying down his life?
4. Does Paul see this present world or heaven as the "real world"?

WISDOM:

1. How can parents apply the principles of this passage to laying down their lives for their children?
2. Is there any guarantee that children will appreciate everything you do?

NOTES

_____

_____

_____

_____

_____

_____

_____

_____

_____

_____

_____

_____

_____

Week Ten—Day Four

Promises

KNOWLEDGE:

Isaiah 48:16-19

Come near me and listen to this:
  "From the first announcement I have not spoken in secret;
  at the time it happens, I am there."
  And now the Sovereign Lord has sent me,
  with his Spirit.

This is what the Lord says—
  your Redeemer, the Holy One of Israel:
  "I am the Lord your God,
  who teaches you what is best for you,
  who directs you in the way you should go.

If only you had paid attention to my commands,
  your peace would have been like a river,
  your righteousness like the waves of the sea.

Your descendants would have been like the sand,
  your children like its numberless grains;
  their name would never be cut off
  nor destroyed from before me."

Joel 2:12-13

Rend Your Heart
"Even now," declares the Lord,
  "return to me with all your heart,
  with fasting and weeping and mourning."
Rend your heart
  and not your garments.
  Return to the Lord your God,

for he is gracious and compassionate,
slow to anger and abounding in love,
and he relents from sending calamity.

Joel 2:25-27

I will repay you for the years the locusts have eaten—
the great locust and the young locust,
the other locusts and the locust swarm—
my great army that I sent among you.

You will have plenty to eat, until you are full,
and you will praise the name of the LORD your God,
who has worked wonders for you;
never again will my people be shamed.

Then you will know that I am in Israel,
that I am the LORD your God,
and that there is no other;
never again will my people be shamed.

UNDERSTANDING:

1. List the promises God makes in these passages.
2. Is it ever too late to repent?
3. What will God do about the devastation you may already have suffered?

WISDOM:

We can never go back in time to re-do a portion of our lives. However, God lives in the eternal present. Every moment that has ever happened or will ever happen is present before him. He can intervene to change the effects of the bad things in our lives. He does not do this for unbelievers. Memorize Romans 8:28—"And we know that in all things God works for the good of those who love him, who have been called according to his purpose."

NOTES

_____

_____

_____

_____

_____

_____

_____

_____

_____

_____

_____

_____

_____

_____

_____

_____

WEEK TEN—DAY FIVE

Exhortation

KNOWLEDGE:

1 Timothy 6:11-20

Paul's Charge to Timothy

But you, man of God, flee from all this, and pursue righteousness, godliness, faith, love, endurance and gentleness. Fight the good fight of the faith. Take hold of the eternal life to which you were called when you made your good confession in the presence of many witnesses. In the sight of God, who gives life to everything, and of Christ Jesus, who while testifying before Pontius Pilate made the good confession, I charge you to keep this command without spot or blame until the appearing of our Lord Jesus Christ, which God will bring about in his own time—God, the blessed and only Ruler, the King of kings and Lord of lords, who alone is immortal and who lives in unapproachable light, whom no one has seen or can see. To him be honor and might forever. Amen.

Command those who are rich in this present world not to be arrogant nor to put their hope in wealth, which is so uncertain, but to put their hope in God, who richly provides us with everything for our enjoyment. Command them to do good, to be rich in good deeds, and to be generous and willing to share. In this way they will lay up treasure for themselves as a firm foundation for the coming age, so that they may take hold of the life that is truly life.

Timothy, guard what has been entrusted to your care. Turn away from godless chatter and the opposing ideas of what is falsely called knowledge, which some have professed and in so doing have wandered from the faith. Grace be with you.

UNDERSTANDING:

1. What is Paul warning Timothy to flee from?
2. For what are we and our children to be laying up treasures?
3. How does Paul confirm once again that this present life is not the true life, that our training is for the life to come?
4. What has been entrusted to Timothy's care?

WISDOM:

1. In what ways can parents guard the children that have been entrusted to their care?
2. What must we turn our children away from?
3. What happens to those who embrace "what is falsely called knowledge"?

NOTES

APPENDIX

German Court Keeps Five Kids Because Parents Are Homeschoolers

A HOMESCHOOLING FAMILY IN Southern Germany spent six hours in a grueling German Family Court session this week with the hopes of regaining custody of their six homeschooled children, who have been held in state custody since January. After the long and confusing session, the Gorbers regained custody of their 3-year-old son. The judge, meanwhile, retained custody of five other Gorber children now being kept in foster care and youth homes pending a court-ordered psychological evaluation of the parents. The court did allow increased visitation for some of the children, up from one hour every two weeks that had been permitted since the children were seized in a surprise raid by the youth welfare office ("Jugendamt") and police.

In January of 2008, Jugendamt and police officials surrounded the German home of the family while Mr. Gorber visited his wife at a local hospital where she had been admitted due to complications from her pregnancy with her ninth child. The oldest son, age 21, and a daughter, age 20, were not taken by the authorities, but all the other children were removed despite their repeated protests.

The siblings reported that the 7-year-old was gripped around the waist by a youth home music teacher, dragged kicking and screaming across the courtyard and thrown into a van. The terrified 3-year-old clung to his 20-year-old sister so tightly that even the police and Jugendamt could not separate them. Both had to be taken to the youth home, where at last the little fellow's strength gave out and he could be taken into custody.

The children then received psychological exams, which all reported that they were normal and well-functioning. Although these evaluations attested to appropriate parenting, the judge indicated that he was unwilling to allow the other children, all of school age, to return home because he did not believe the father's assurances that he would enroll the children in school.

Someone who attended the six-hour hearing described the scene as "bedlam in the courtroom, without any attempt by the judge to impose discipline. The parties kept interrupting each other and everyone spoke at once." Some of the children have reported that their court-appointed attorneys said they will fight to keep them in foster care despite the children's firmly stated desire to return home to their parents.

Many in Europe are critical of Germany's Jugendamt. Germany has Europe's highest incidence of removing children from their homes. A recent article in Germany's Zeitung newspaper showed figures indicating that the removal of children from their homes was up 12.5% this year in Germany, while the number of abused children remained the same.

Opponents have accused the child welfare system in Germany of corruption, driven by exorbitant payments by the government to children's homes and foster care providers. This "youth welfare industry" is financed by a 21 billion euro budget. The local operating youth welfare committees include privately owned and for-profit children's care institutions who participate with legal sanction on the committees with two-fifths of the total vote. No other child welfare system in the world is known to allow this type of intermingling between government and commercial enterprises. Such an intermingling would appear to create a serious conflict of interest.

Appendix: German Court Keeps Five Kids Because Parents Are Homeschoolers

This is of particular concern to homeschooling families in Germany in light of court decisions and a recent change to the federal youth welfare law that was signed by German President Roland Koch on July 5 of this year. The law, BGB 1666, establishes the standard by which family courts are to determine whether custody of parents can be taken away. The law was changed to make it easier for children to be removed by the Jugendamt when the children are "endangered." But endangerment is not defined in the law. The highest German courts have ruled that homeschooling is not tolerated because it creates "parallel societies" and is an abuse of parent's rights. Administrative agencies and courts have stated that the failure to send children to school is by definition "endangerment."

Until last year, homeschooling families had mostly been harassed with exorbitant fines. This year, however, Rosemarie and Juergen Dudek of Archfeldt, Germany, were sentenced to three months each in prison for homeschooling. In a previous family court case involving the Dudeks, the judge declined to take away the parental rights of the parents. It was thought that the Dudeks cared for and educated their children too well to justify penal removal of the children under the legal clause "misuse of parental authority." During the Dudek's criminal trial, the judge ordered a 900 euro fine against the family for not sending their children to school. Not satisfied with this "lenient" sentence, local State Prosecutor Herwig Mueller told Mr. Dudek, "You won't have to worry about paying the fine, because I'm going to send you to jail." His appeal of the fine resulted in the latest prison sentence for Mr. and Mrs. Dudek.

More homeschooling families have fled Germany as a result of this persecution, as it now appears that family court judges and the Jugendamt are ready and willing to take children away from their parents simply because they are being homeschooled. Nevertheless, "We are greatly encouraged by the thoughts and prayers of American homeschoolers," said Mr. Dudek in a recent phone conversation with HSLDA Staff Attorney Michael Donnelly. "It gives us hope to know that there are people who have the freedom to educate their own children at home.

We so appreciate the letters and notes of encouragement. These letters help us maintain our focus and in seeking God's will for our family."

These cases are drawing attention within Germany and across Europe. Kathy Sinnott, a European parliament member from Ireland, criticized Germany's treatment of homeschooling and the way the Jugendamt treats non-German families residing in Germany. In a recent press release, Sinnot said, "Germany's approach to homeschooling compromises this [European law on mobility] and forces families to choose between a job and the best interests of the children. The need for family-friendly employment policies must be recognized throughout the EU. We need to have flexibility in the education of children temporarily resident because of work. There is also an issue around the attitude to non-German families in the German children's courts. I hope the dialogue between the Commission and the German State will resolve this discriminatory situation."

A member of the SPD party in Bavaria, Germany, also stated in a recent radio interview that "imprisonment or fines in this matter are absolutely excessive in my opinion, because homeschooling can provide very high-quality outcomes. This topic is definitely one which we must work through politically. There can be no black-white declarations, but we must discuss this without ideological blinders on." Although encouraging, it will take more than one or two members of state legislatures to effect the needed change.

Donnelly, during a recent trip to Germany to encourage homeschoolers and to work for change, met with the Gorber family as well as with policy and lawmakers at the European Union and in the German State of Baden Wurttemberg.

"This poor, simple family is being crushed by unbearable pressure from the German state's police power, primarily because they are homeschoolers," Donnelly said. "This father of nine, a woodworker, told me how difficult this is and the incredible strain it's placing on his children, his wife and himself. As longtime homeschoolers, they have irritated the local youth authorities who needed only the pretext of the hospitalization of the mother and other exaggerated claims to seize the children." Donnelly noted that "while there are some policy makers in some of the states who are willing to take on this important issue of human rights, most couldn't be bothered. It is going to take increased public awareness and international pressure to confront German society with this outrageous behavior. Unfortunately, it looks like more parents will have to go to jail and more children taken into state custody before German public policy makers wake up and do something. It's very disturbing that Germany can get away with this kind of behavior with such little public comment by other Western governments."

HSLDA is committed to working with national and international ministries and associations to support German homeschoolers in their fight to be free from persecution. The right of parents to direct the upbringing and education of their children is a fundamental human right, and HSLDA is grateful for the support of its members to defend this freedom here in the United States and abroad.

* Report from Home School Legal Defense Association on August 1, 2008 www.hslda.org/hs/international/Germany/20080801.asp

For more information about the Home School Legal Defense Association, go to www.hslda.org.

In memory of
my parents
Bud and Lori Van Zuidam
and my brother
David Van Zuidam

Endnotes

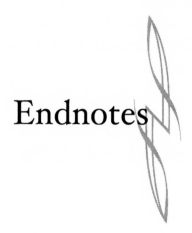

1. Dobson, Dr. James and Gary Bauer. *Children At Risk, 22.* Dallas, Texas: WORD Publishing, 1990.

2. Maddoux, Marlin. *Public Education Against America: the Hidden Agenda,*169-173. New Kensington, PA: Whitaker House, 2006.

3. Pearcey, Nancy. *Total Truth*, 23. Wheaton Illinois: Crossway Books, 2004.

4. Schaeffer, Francis. *How Should We Then Live?*, 19-20. Westchester, Illinois: Crossway Books, 1976.

5. Van Til, Cornelius. "Antithesis is Education." In *Foundations of Christian Education: Addresses to Christian Teachers*, by Louis and Cornelius Van Til Berkhof, 7-8. Phillipsburg, New Jersey: Presbyterian and Reformed Publishing Company, 1953; reprinted in 1990.

6. Pearcey, Nancy. *Total Truth*, 43. Wheaton Illinois: Crossway Books, 2004.

7. Lewis, C.S. *The Abolition of Man*, 16-17. New York, New York: Macmillan Publishing Company, 1947.

8. Berkhof, Louis. "Being Reformed in Our Attitude Toward Christian School." In *Foundations of Christian Education: Addresses to Christian*

Teachers, by Louis and Cornelius Van Til Berkhof, edited by Dennis E. Johnson, p.32. Phillipsburg, New Jersey: Presbyterian and Reformed Publishing Company, 1953; reprinted in 1990.

9. Ibid.

10. American Family Association. "It's Not Gay" Produced by Don Wildmon. DVD available at www.afa.net.

11. Ibid.

12. Voltaire, Francois Marie Arouet de. *Letters Concerning the English Nation*. Buffalo, New York: University of Tortonto Press, 1733. Quoted in *How Should We Then Live?* by Francis Schaeffer, 120-121. Westchester, Illinois: Crossway Books, 1976.

13. Schaeffer, Francis. *How Should We Then Live?*, 126. Westchester, Illinois: Crossway Books, 1976.

14. Ibid.

15. The *Humanist Manifesto 2* can be viewed in its entirety at the following webpage: "What is Humanism?" *Humanist Manifesto 2*. 1933. http://www.jcn.com/manifestos.html (accessed August 25, 2008). Bold highlighting is mine.

16. For a comprehensive analysis of public school texts, read *Dreamers of a Godless Utopia: How to Recognize Worldview Bias in Education* by Michael J. Chapman. This book includes the "History of the Ideological Shift in Education" and the complete Humanist Manifestos 1 and 2. See also www.AmericanHeritageResearch.org and www.EdWatch.org.

17. Shirer. *The Rise and Fall of the Third Reich: A History of Nazi Germany*, 249. New York: Simon and Schuster, 1959.

18. Dobson, Dr. James and Gary Bauer. *Children At Risk, 37-39*. Dallas, Texas: WORD Publishing, 1990.

19. Sources for the history of public education include:
Chapman, Michael. "The Ideological Shift in American Education: Humanism vs. Biblical Worldview: a chronology." In *Dreamers of a Godless Utopia: How to Recognize Worldview Bias in*

Education, by Chapman, A3. Chapman, 2006. (available at www. AmericanHeritageResearch.com)

Gatto, John Taylor. *The Underground History of American Education.* Oxford, New York: The Oxford Village Press, Revised Ed. 2006.

Maddoux, Marlin. *Public Education Against America: the Hidden Agenda.* New Kensington, PA: Whitaker House, 2006.

A comprehensive chronology of events/publications, etc. compiled in book form by **Dennis L. Cuddy, Ph.D.,** one time official with the US Department of Education in Washington is available by sending $13.45 to *Pro Family Forum, Inc., P.O. Box 1059, Highland City, FL 33846-1059.*

20. Quoted in Popper, Karl R. *The Open Society and Its Enemies,* vol. 2 p. 31,*4th ed. 2 vols.* Princeton, NJ: Princeton University Press, 1963,

21. Chapman, Michael. "The Ideological Shift in American Education: Humanism vs. Biblical Worldview: a chronology." In *Dreamers of a Godless Utopia: How to Recognize Worldview Bias in Education*, by Chapman, A3. Chapman, 2006.

22. Maddoux, Marlin. *Public Education Against America: the Hidden Agenda, 99.* New Kensington, PA: Whitaker House, 2006.

23. Ibid., 106.

24. Cubberly, Ellwood in *Changing Conceptions of Education.* Quoted in Gatto, John Taylor. *The Underground History of American Education, 331.* Oxford, New York: The Oxford Village Press, Revised Ed. 2006.

25. *World History: The Human Journey,* 564-567. Published by Holt, Rinehart and Winston. 2003.

26. Chapman, Michael. "The Ideological Shift in American Education: Humanism vs. Biblical Worldview: a chronology." In *Dreamers of a Godless Utopia: How to Recognize Worldview Bias in Education*, by Chapman, A3. Chapman, 2006.

27. Gatto, John Taylor. *The Underground History of American Education, 61-62.* Oxford, New York: The Oxford Village Press, Revised Ed. 2006.

28. Ibid., 46.

29. Maddoux, Marlin. *Public Education Against America: the Hidden Agenda*, 155-159. New Kensington, PA: Whitaker House, 2006.

30. Thomas Sowell is an American economist, political writer, and commentator. He is currently a senior fellow of the Hoover Institution at Stanford University. In 2002 he was awarded the National Humanities Medal for prolific scholarship and melding history, economics, and political science.

31. Quoted in Maddoux, Marlin. *Public Education Against America: the Hidden Agenda,* 134. New Kensington, PA: Whitaker House, 2006.

32. Bold highlighting is mine.

33. Summary of *TOUGH CHOICES OR TOUGH TIMES* NCEE. *TOUGH CHOICES OR TOUGH TIMES.* San Francisco, CA: Jossey-Bass, 2008. The summary is available at www.skillscommission.org.

34. Ibid.

35. Satan was quoting Psalm 91, which promises God's protection for the righteous. This protection does not apply when we are acting outside the boundaries of God's will.

36. The story of Jehoshaphat and his descendents can be found in 1 Kings 22 and 2 Chronicles 17-22.

37. Quoted in Federer, William J. ed. *America's God and Country Encyclopedia of Quotations.* Coppell, Texas: Fame Publications, 1994.

38. Ninth Circuit Court of Appeals. "Alliance for the Separation of School and State." *The Case for Separation.* March 28, 2008. www.schoolandstate.org/Case/parentsoffaith.htm (accessed August 25, 2008).

39. Voltaire. *Brainy Quote.* 2008. www.brainyquote.com/quotes/quotes/v/voltaire169602.html (accessed August 25, 2008).

40. Maddoux, Marlin. *Public Education Against America: the Hidden Agenda,* 123-136. New Kensington, PA: Whitaker House, 2006.

41. *Our Nation*, 126-7. Published by Macmillan/McGraw-Hill, 2003.

42. Maddoux, Marlin. *Public Education Against America: The Hidden Agenda,* 141-142. New Kensington, PA: Whitaker House. 2006.

43. McDowell, Sean. "Apologetics 4 @ New Generation." *Christian Research Journal* Vol. 30 No. 01, p. 25. 2007.

44. Chapman, Michael. *Dreamers of a Godless Utopia: How to Recognize Worldview Bias in Education,* 5. Michael J. Chapman, Revised Ed. 2006.

45. There are no scripture references for these conclusions for good reason: it would spoil your treasure hunt!

46. Baucham, Voddie (Jr.) *The Children of Caesar.* Lecture on DVD. Produced by THE AMERICAN VISION, 2007.

47. Moore, Raymond S. and Nancy N. et al. *School Can Wait,* 101. Washougal, WA: Hewitt Research Foundation, 1982.

48. Ibid., 205-206.

49. Ibid., 214.

50. Ibid.

51. See appendix for the story of one German family.

52. Piper, John. *What Jesus Demands From the World,* 330. Wheaton, Illinois: Crossway Books, 2006.